LAW FOR THE SMALL BUSINESS OWNER

2nd Edition

by
Margaret C. Jasper

Oceana's Legal Almanac Series
Law for the Layperson

2001
Oceana Publications, Inc.
Dobbs Ferry, New York

Library of Congress Control Number: 2001132454

ISBN 0-379-11357-0

Oceana's Legal Almanac Series: Law for the Layperson
ISSN 1075-7376

To My Husband Chris

Your love and support
are my motivation and inspiration

-and-

In memory of my son, Jimmy

Table of Contents

CHAPTER 6:
EMPLOYER/EMPLOYEE RELATIONS

CHAPTER 7:
MAINTAINING BUSINESS RECORDS

CHAPTER 8:
OFFICE EQUIPMENT AND TECHNOLOGY

APPENDICES

ABOUT THE AUTHOR

MARGARET C. JASPER is an attorney engaged in the general practice of law in South Salem, New York, concentrating in the areas of personal injury and entertainment law. Ms. Jasper holds a Juris Doctor degree from Pace University School of Law, White Plains, New York, is a member of the New York and Connecticut bars, and is certified to practice before the United States District Courts for the Southern and Eastern Districts of New York, and the United States Supreme Court.

Ms. Jasper has been appointed to the panel of arbitrators of the American Arbitration Association and the law guardian panel for the Family Court of the State of New York, is a member of the Association of Trial Lawyers of America, and is a New York State licensed real estate broker and member of the Westchester County Board of Realtors, operating as Jasper Real Estate, in South Salem, New York.

Ms. Jasper is the author and general editor of the following legal almanacs: Juvenile Justice and Children's Law; Marriage and Divorce; Estate Planning; The Law of Contracts; The Law of Dispute Resolution; Law for the Small Business Owner; The Law of Personal Injury; Real Estate Law for the Homeowner and Broker; Everyday Legal Forms; Dictionary of Selected Legal Terms; The Law of Medical Malpractice; The Law of Product Liability; The Law of No-Fault Insurance; The Law of Immigration; The Law of Libel and Slander; The Law of Buying and Selling; Elder Law; The Right to Die; AIDS Law; The Law of Obscenity and Pornography; The Law of Child Custody; The Law of Debt Collection; Consumer Rights Law; Bankruptcy Law for the Individual Debtor; Victim's Rights Law; Animal Rights Law; Workers' Compensation Law; Employee Rights in the Workplace; Probate Law; Environmental Law; Labor Law; The Americans with Disabilities Act; The Law of Capital Punishment; Education Law; The Law of Violence Against Women; Landlord-Tenant Law; Insurance Law; Religion and the Law; Commercial Law; Motor Vehicle Law; Social Security Law; The Law of Drunk Driving; The Law of Speech and the First Amendment; Employment Discrimination Under Title VII; Hospital Liability Law; Home Mortgage Law Primer; Copyright Law; Patent Law; Trademark Law; Special Education Law; The Law of Attachment and Garnishment; Banks and their Customers; and Credit Cards and the Law.

INTRODUCTION

Many people, at one time or another, dream of owning their own business—being their own boss. Nobody likes to punch a time clock or worry about the day they may receive that dreaded "pink slip." The security—or the illusion of security—of being an employee, such as receiving a regular salary and periodic salary increases, and the benefits an employee usually enjoys, e.g., medical benefits, vacation pay, and pension plans, deters most workers from pursuing their dreams. However, in these unpredictable economic times, many major corporations have gone under, leaving their faithful, long-term employees without jobs or benefits.

This turn of events has caused many people, either by choice or necessity, to use their skills and knowledge to start up their own businesses. According to the Small Business Administration, new business formation reached a record level in 1998. An estimated 898,000 new firms with employees opened their doors—a 1.5 percent increase over the record 885,000 begun in 1997. Interest in owning or starting a small business has broken new records over the last five years and part-time entrepreneurs have increased dramatically. Sixty percent of these new firms began at home.

Working for a weekly paycheck can never be as rewarding as the income one receives from undertaking a successful business venture. Nevertheless, establishing a new business is statistically very risky, although the statistics are improving. According to the Small Business Administration, of every seven businesses that shut their doors, only one actually fails, leaving unpaid obligations. The remainder close for voluntary reasons, such as a desire to enter a new field, or for personal health or other reasons. Business bankruptcies declined by 17.9 percent, from 53,843 in 1997 to 44,005 in 1998. The 1998 level represents a record low share of bankruptcies and the lowest number since 1981, when the total number of businesses was much smaller.

Further, small businesses continue to be the keystone of the U.S. economy. Small businesses with fewer than 500 workers employ 53 percent of the private nonfarm work force, contribute 47 percent of all sales in the country, and are responsible for 51 percent of the private gross domestic product. Industries dominated by small firms contributed a major share of the 3.1 million new jobs created in 1998. Over the 1990-1995 period, small firms with fewer than 500 employees created 76 percent of net new jobs. Small businesses produce 55 percent of innovations and are responsible for such major technological advances as the airplane, the heart valve, the pacemaker, and the personal computer.

This legal almanac explores all of the major aspects of establishing and managing the small business. It presents data on the demographic characteristics of small business in the United States today. It also defines and discusses the various types of businesses one may choose to organize. It explores the practical problems one may face in setting up a business, such as choosing the best location and equipment, handling the finances, keeping proper records, and entering the competitive world of electronic commerce. Finally, this almanac examines the employer-employee relationship, and discusses the legal obligations which arise from this relationship.

The Appendix provides sample documents and other pertinent information and data. The Glossary contains definitions of many of the basic legal terms used throughout the almanac.

CHAPTER 1:
DEMOGRAPHIC CHARACTERISTICS OF SMALL BUSINESSES

SMALL BUSINESS FACTS AND STATISTICS

There are approximately 25 million small businesses in the United States.

In 1998, seven of the 10 industries which added the most new jobs were in sectors dominated by small businesses.

Small businesses provide approximately 75 percent of the net new jobs added to the economy and provide 67 percent of workers with their first jobs.

Small businesses represent 99.7 percent of all employers.

Small businesses employ 53 percent of the private work force.

Small businesses provide 47 percent of all sales in the country.

Small businesses provide 55 percent of innovations.

Small businesses account for 35 percent of federal contract dollars.

Small businesses account for 38 percent of jobs in high technology sectors.

Small businesses account for 51 percent of private sector output.

Small businesses represent 96 percent of all U.S. exporters.

Of the 5,369,068 employer businesses in 1995, 78.8 percent had fewer than 10 employees, and 99.7 percent had fewer than 500 employees.

Part-time employment was 20.5 percent of the small business work force, and 17.4 percent of the large business work force in 1996.

Small businesses employed a higher percentage of workers under age 25 and workers aged 65 and over than did large businesses in 1996.

Of small business workers, 53.7 percent had an education of a high school degree or less, compared with 44.3 percent of large business workers in 1996.

The percentage of full-time employees in small business employer pension plans increased 12.9 percent from 1992 to 1996.

Of the 11.3 million self-employed individuals with earnings in 1996, 37.4 percent were women, 6.0 percent were black, 5.9 percent had Hispanic origins, 54.5 percent were aged 35 to 54, 75.1 percent earned less than $25,000 and 43.0 percent were in service industries.

Of all of the businesses in 1992, 73.0 percent were started by original founders, compared to 29.8 percent for businesses with 100 or more employees.

Of the businesses without employees in 1992, 27.0 percent were started within the last two years, compared with 9.7 percent of businesses with 1 to 4 employees.

Of all of the businesses in 1992, 56.5 percent were home-based when first established, 3.1 percent were franchises, and 75.5 percent of the businesses in 1992 survived until at least 1996.

According to the Small Business Administration, small businesses generally provide more initial on-the-job training, and are more likely to employ younger and older workers, former welfare recipients, and women, many of whom prefer or are able to work only on a part-time basis.

WOMEN AND SMALL BUSINESS

Growth

Women-owned businesses are a vital part of our nation's successful economy. They outpace other small business sectors in growth and participate in every industry. The U.S. Small Business Administration's Office of Advocacy estimates that there were 8.5 million women-owned businesses in 1997, accounting for more than one-third of all businesses. Their numbers have been increasing steadily, and more rapidly, than other small businesses in the economy by 89 percent over the last decade compared with a 29 percent increase in the total number of businesses. Women-owned businesses generated $3.1 trillion in revenues, up 209 percent between 1987 and 1997, after adjusting for inflation.

By 1997, the number of self-employed women increased 48 percent compared with an increase of just 1.5 percent for men. It is estimated that about 4.7 million women will be self-employed by 2005, up 77 percent from 1983, compared with a 6 percent increase in self-employed men.

By state, women's share of self-employment ranged from a low of 28 percent in Rhode Island to more than 46 percent in Arizona. In 13 states and the District of Columbia, more than 40 percent of self-employed persons were women. The top 5 states are Arizona, Colorado, Hawaii, Wyoming and the District of Columbia. States having the highest growth rates of women-owned businesses were Florida, Georgia, Idaho, Nevada and New Mexico, states which have also experienced the highest growth in business overall.

A chart demonstrating women's share of self-employment, by state, is set forth at Appendix 1.

Employment

Women-owned businesses have contributed significantly to the nation's economy by creating jobs and employing approximately 23.8 million people—a 262 percent increase over the 1987-1997 period. The number of women-owned businesses with employees grew by 46 percent from 1987 to 1997. In 1992, more than 14 percent of women owned businesses had paid employees compared with 16 percent of all businesses.

Types of Businesses

Of the 5.8 million women-owned businesses, excluding C corporations, in 1992, 53.7 percent were in services. Women were most represented in retail trade, encompassing 44 percent of the market. In 1992, 3.5 percent of all women-owned businesses and 16 percent of those with 20-100 employees were franchises. Women own about 10 percent of franchised businesses. Only 10.2 percent of women-owned businesses are in finance, life insurance and real estate.

Women-owned businesses are least represented in the construction, wholesale trade, manufacturing, public utilities, mining, and agricultural markets. However, over the 1987-1992 period, women-owned businesses increased fastest in these capital-intensive industries. Nevertheless, only 1.7 percent of federal prime contract dollars went to women-owned businesses in 1996 despite the fact that women-owned businesses represent about one-third of all businesses in the United States and more than 11 percent of all business revenue.

According to the U.S. Census Bureau, women own about 36.9 percent of the more than 9 million home-based businesses. More than 60 percent of women-owned businesses were first operated in the home and 58 percent were still operated in the residence in 1992. Businesses that remained small were much more likely to continue to be home-based. Only 29.9 percent of all women-owned businesses with employees began in the home with 22.6 percent of those businesses still operating from the home in 1992.

Financing

To finance their business, one-half of all women-owned businesses used some type of traditional loan and 60 percent used nontraditional sources such as finance companies and personal credit cards. Although commercial banks were the traditional financing source used most often by women, only 32 percent of women-owned businesses used them in 1993. The type of traditional financing most used by women-owned businesses were for vehicle loans, equipment loans, and lines of credit. Nearly three-quarters of all women-owned businesses accessed some type of credit in 1993. More than 35 percent of all women-owned businesses used some type of credit card for their business credit needs in 1993. A higher than average of 10 percent of women-owned businesses rely on family and friends for financing the business.

MINORITIES AND SMALL BUSINESS

Defined

On a Federal level, Congress considers a minority-owned business as generally anyone other than white. The business must be owned and at least 51% controlled by one or more minorities. Women are not considered minorities. It is a self-certifying process and no paperwork needs to be filled out. However, your state and local government may have different rules and regulations regarding their contracts and their definition of a minority-owned business. Therefore, the reader is advised to consult their state and local government rules and requirements in this regard.

Growth

Minority-owned businesses are an important part of our nation's economy, participating in many industries. According to the Small Business Administration Office of Advocacy, there has been a significant increase in minority-owned small businesses. Over the 1987-1997 decade, the number of minority-owned businesses increased 168 percent to about 3.25 million by 1997. Minority-owned businesses generated $495 billion in revenues in 1997, up 343 percent from 1987, adjusted for inflation, and employed almost 4 million workers.

Of the 11.5 million people with some self-employment earnings in 1997, about 5.8 percent were Hispanic, 5.8 percent African American, and 4.5 percent Asian and other.

A chart demonstrating self-employment by race and ethnic origin from 1988 through 1998 is set forth at Appendix 2.

Of all businesses in existence in 1992, 75.5 percent were still in existence by 1996. This compares with 74.3 percent of Hispanic-owned businesses, 68.9 percent of African-American-owned businesses, and 79.2 percent of Asian and other minority-owned businesses.

Hispanic and Asian-owned businesses have increased most dramatically as compared to African-American-owned businesses. This may be attributed to immigration since historically new settlers in this country have initially earned their living by starting new small businesses.

African-American-Owned Businesses

The number of African-American-owned businesses increased 108 percent from 1987 to 1997 to 881,646. Their revenues were up 109 percent, adjusted for inflation. African-American-owned businesses made up 27.4 percent of all minority-owned businesses in 1997. In 1998, self-employment was the primary occupation of 533,500 African-Americans, representing a 28 percent growth over the decade.

Approximately 57 percent of all African-American-owned businesses began as home-based businesses. Nearly 70 percent of African-American business owners are between the ages of 25 and 54, more than 90 percent of whom were born in the United States.

The five states with the highest number of African-American-owned businesses as of 1992 were California, New York, Texas, Florida, and Georgia. States having the highest growth rates of African-American-owned businesses were North Dakota, Minnesota, Georgia, Hawaii and Maine.

Hispanic-Owned Businesses

The number of Hispanic-owned businesses increased 232 percent from 1987 to 1997 to an estimated 1.4 million. Their revenues increased 417 percent adjusted for inflation. Hispanic-owned businesses made up nearly 44 percent of all minority-owned businesses in 1997, up from 34.8 percent in 1987. In 1998, self-employment was the primary occupation of 661,000 Hispanics, representing a 30 percent growth over the decade.

Approximately 51.6 of all Hispanic-owned businesses began as home-based businesses. More than 75 percent of Hispanic business owners are between the ages of 25 and 54, one-half of whom were born in the United States.

The five states with the highest number of Hispanic-owned businesses as of 1992 were California, Texas, Florida, New York, and New Jersey. States having the highest growth rates of Hispanic-owned businesses were Maine, North Carolina, Rhode Island, Vermont and Tennessee.

Asian, Pacific Islander, American Indian, and Alaskan Aleut-Owned Businesses

The number of Asian and other minority-owned businesses increased 180 percent from 1987 to 1997 to about 1.1 million. Their revenues grew 463 percent, adjusted for inflation, to $275 billion. Asian and other minority-owned businesses made up 32.9 percent of all minority-owned businesses in 1997, a slight increase over the 31 percent share in 1987. Asian-owned businesses grew the fastest individually and as a group as compared to other minority-owned businesses. In 1998, self-employment was the primary occupation of 460,000 Asians, representing a 56.5 percent growth over the decade.

Only 37.6 percent of all Asian-owned businesses began as home-based businesses as compared to the national average of 56.5 percent of home-based business start-ups. Approximately 75 percent of Asian business owners were between the ages of 25 and 54, less than one-third of whom were born in the United States.

The five states with the highest number of Asian-owned businesses as of 1992 were California, New York, Texas, Hawaii, and New Jersey. States having the highest growth rates of Asian-owned businesses were Vermont, New Mexico, Georgia, Rhode Island and Maine.

Employment

Of the 3.25 million minority-owned businesses, more than 520,000 had employees in 1997, up 111 percent from 1987. An estimated 3.9 million employees worked for minority-owned businesses in 1997, an increase of 362 percent from 1987.

African-American Owned Businesses

The number of African-American-owned businesses with employees grew just 27 percent over the 1987-1997 decade, but their revenues were up 127 percent, adjusted for inflation. More than 580,000 employees worked for African-American-owned businesses in 1997, up 165 percent over the previous decade.

Hispanic-Owned Businesses

Of Hispanic-owned businesses, more than 200,000 had employees in 1997, up 144 percent from 1987. Their revenues grew 529 percent over the period to $160 billion. The number of employees working for Hispanic-owned businesses grew 464 percent over the decade to 1.5 million workers.

Asian, Pacific Islander, American Indian, and Alaskan Aleut-Owned Businesses

Nearly 250,000 of these businesses had employees, up 157 percent between 1987 and 1997. They generated $245 billion in revenues, up 580 percent over the period. The number of employees working for these businesses grew 432 percent from 1987 to 1997, to 1.9 million workers.

Types of Businesses

From 1987 to 1992, the fastest growing industry for African-Americans was in services. Hispanic and Asian-owned businesses grew fastest in finance, insurance, and real estate. In 1992, approximately 3 percent of all businesses were franchises whereas more than 4 percent of African-American-owned businesses and almost 5 percent of Asian-owned businesses were franchises. The number of Hispanic-owned franchise businesses fell slightly below the national average.

Notably, Hispanic and Asian-owned businesses have an above-average share of the businesses that export goods and services as compared to all businesses. In 1992, only 1.8 percent of all businesses engaged in exporting, compared to 2.5 percent of Hispanic-owned businesses and 2.3 percent of Asian-owned businesses. This may be attributed to strong ties by these groups to their original countries whereas African-Americans have had little immigration in recent decades and account for less than 1 percent of business exports.

Of the 195 million dollars of prime federal contract dollars available in 1997, 5.6 percent went to minority-owned businesses.

Financing

According to the 1993 National Survey of Small Business Finances, 75.7 percent of all small businesses, 69.9 percent of Hispanic-owned, 63.3 percent of African-American-owned, and 67 percent of all minority-owned small businesses, including Asian, used some type of credit.

Commercial banks were a business credit source used by 36.9 percent of all businesses and by 32.6 percent of Hispanic-owned, 15.4 percent of African-American-owned, and 26.6 percent of all minority-owned businesses. About 45-50 percent of all minority-owned businesses used credit cards in 1998.

Although commercial banks were the traditional financing source used most often by minority-owned businesses, only 26.6 percent of minority-owned businesses used them in 1993. The type of traditional financing most used by minority-owned business were for vehicle loans, equipment loans, and lines of credit. More than one-quarter of minority-owned businesses used business credit cards and 36 percent used personal credit cards for all or part of their credit needs.

FASTEST GROWING SMALL BUSINESSES

The fastest growing small business dominated industries over the past several years have included computer programming and management consulting services, residential building construction, job training services, amusement and recreation services, credit reporting and investment firms, providers of day care, and counseling and rehabilitation services.

According to recent projections, small business dominated sectors will contribute about 60 percent of new jobs from 1994 to 2005. About 88 percent of the new jobs will be in retail trade or services. Among the fastest growing small business dominated sectors over this period will be medical and dental laboratories (up 84 percent), residential care industries (up 83 percent), credit reporting (up 68 percent), equipment leasing (up 51 percent), child day care services (up 59 percent), and job training (up 43 percent).

Jobs in high-paying service sectors including offices of physicians and architectural and engineering services will rise about 30 percent. The restaurant industry is projected to add 1.02 million new jobs from 1994 to 2005.

PROFILE OF THE SUCCESSFUL ENTREPRENEUR

One of the first questions the potential entrepreneur asks is whether he or she can handle owning and managing a small business. It is essential that this question be answered realistically and objectively before choosing to start a business. Thoroughly and objectively evaluate your strengths and weaknesses, physical and mental capabilities, personal financial situation, and personal life. Keep in mind that running a small business can be a demanding, frustrating and time-consuming endeavor, and necessarily requires strong family support.

Since the success or demise of your business rests primarily on your shoulders, you must be determined to do everything necessary to support the business. Some personality traits which are particularly advantageous to the entrepreneur include:

1. Strong drive and motivation

2. The ability to get along with a variety of personalities

3. Good decision-making capabilities

4. Good planning and organizational skills

Some personality warning signs that may indicate an inability to succeed in small business are:

1. Laziness

2. Disorganization

3. Emotional instability

4. Lack of physical stamina

5. Lack of motivation

6. Inability to get along with others

7. Indecisiveness

8. Impatience

9. Frustration

10. Excessive dependence on others

If you have exhibited one or more of the above traits in your past endeavors, you may want to work on that aspect of your personality before investing your time and money in a small business.

CHAPTER 2:
THE SMALL BUSINESS ADMINISTRATION

IN GENERAL

America's 25 million small businesses employ more than 50 percent of the private work force, generate more than half of the nation's gross domestic product, and are the principal source of new jobs in the United States economy. In 1953, recognizing the importance of small businesses to the economy of the United States, Congress created the Small Business Administration (SBA). The SBA is a federal government agency which offers financing, training and advocacy for small business owners. In addition, the SBA works with thousands of lending, educational and training institutions nationwide.

With a portfolio of business loans, loan guarantees and disaster loans worth more than $45 billion, in addition to a venture capital portfolio of $13 billion, the SBA is the nation's largest single financial backer of small businesses. Last year, the SBA offered management and technical assistance to more than one million small business owners. The SBA also plays a major role in the government's disaster relief efforts by making low-interest recovery loans to both homeowners and businesses.

The SBA has offices in every state to help America's entrepreneurs form successful small enterprises. You may also visit the SBA on the World Wide Web at http://www.sba.gov/regions/states.html.

A list of the SBA's national district offices is set forth at Appendix 3.

THE SBA INFORMATION ANSWER DESK

The SBA also operates a telephone service for small business owners called the "SBA Information Answer Desk." The Answer Desk is the only national toll-free telephone service providing information to the public on small business problems and concerns. This service provides general information about SBA programs and other programs available to assist the small business community. The Answer Desk office also has a comprehensive listing of SBA publications. SBA Business Information Assistants are available between the hours of 9:00 AM and 5:00 PM (EST).

If you have questions about SBA programs, or would like information on local resource groups, please email your request to answer desk@sba.gov.

The SBA Answer Desk can be reached as follows:

Answer Desk
200 North College Street, Suite A-2015
Charlotte, North Carolina 28202
Telephone: 1-800-UASK-SBA (1-800-827-5722)
Email Address: answer desk@sba.gov

SBA PROGRAMS

The Small Business Administration has a variety of programs to assist the small business owner. It offers free one-on-one counseling to help entre-preneurs and potential entrepreneurs in the areas of financing, manage-ment technology, government procurement, and other business related areas. Other available SBA programs and services include training and edu-cational programs, advisory services, publications, and financial and con-tract assistance.

The SBA offers a variety of loans and financial assistance to eligible small businesses, particularly those who have been unsuccessful in acquiring outside financing. The SBA offers specialized programs for women busi-ness owners, minorities, veterans, international trade, and rural develop-ment. The majority of SBA's business loans are made by private lenders with partial guarantees by SBA.

The SBA also expands access to surety bonds through guarantees on bonding for small and new contractors, including minority contractors, who otherwise would not be able to secure bid, payment, or performance bonds. The SBA will guarantee to a qualified surety up to 80% of losses in-curred under bid, payment, or performance bonds issued to contractors on contracts valued up to 1.25 million dollars. In addition, the SBA monitors the federal agencies to assist small businesses in securing a percentage of federal contract awards.

The SBA also offers a full range of special loan programs, including:

1. International trade loan guarantees to finance U.S. based facilities or equipment for producing goods or services for export;

2. Export revolving line of credit guarantees to help businesses penetrate foreign markets;

3. Small loan guarantees to help businesses needing capital of $50,000 or less;

4. Small general contractor loan guarantees for small construction businesses;

5. Seasonal line of credit guarantees for businesses facing seasonal business increases;

6. Energy loan guarantees for businesses that make, install, sell, or service energy equipment and technology;

7. Handicapped assistance loans for businesses owned by physically handicapped persons and private nonprofit organizations that employ handicapped persons and operate in their interest;

8. Pollution control loan guarantees for businesses involved in pollution control and reduction; and

9. Loans to disabled and Vietnam veterans to start, operate or expand a small business.

THE SERVICE CORPS OF RETIRED EXECUTIVES (SCORE)

In addition to its direct services, the SBA sponsors the Service Corps of Retired Executives (SCORE), a training and counseling service. SCORE offers free, expert advise and confidential counseling from approximately 13,000 experienced business professionals from a variety of backgrounds on virtually every aspect of business.

There are 380 SCORE chapter locations around the country and an additional 380 branch locations.

For further information about SCORE, contact the National SCORE Office at:

Service Corps of Retired Executives (SCORE)
409 Third St., S.W., Suite 5900
Washington, DC 20024
Telephone: 1-800-634-0245

SMALL BUSINESS DEVELOPMENT CENTERS (SBDCS)

The SBA operates approximately 1,000 Small Business Development Centers (SBDC) nationwide. The SBDC provides a variety of management and technical assistance services to small businesses and potential entrepreneurs.

SMALL BUSINESS INVESTMENT COMPANIES (SBICS)

The SBA licenses, regulates, and invests in privately owned and managed Small Business Investment Companies (SBICs) across the country, in order to provide small businesses with long-term loans and venture capital.

CHAPTER 3:
ORGANIZING THE BUSINESS

CHOOSING THE TYPE OF BUSINESS

The most important task that must be done before organizing your business is determining what type of business you are capable of managing. One of the biggest mistakes a potential entrepreneur can make is starting a business in a field about which he or she knows nothing, and in which he or she has little or no experience.

The ideal business for the new small business owner is in an area where the person has the most experience. Although past employment in the area is not necessary, it is often the source of experience for many entrepreneurs. In the alternative, the requisite experience can be acquired as a result of a hobby or special interest. Try to learn everything possible about the business you want to start beforehand, because too much will be at stake once you have already begun operations. If your proposed business is so multifaceted that it would be impossible or impractical for you to learn it all, then you must make sure that you bring in key personnel who have the experience and knowledge to compensate for your deficiencies.

You must also ascertain whether there are any particular legal requirements for your proposed business. For example, does your proposed business require any special licenses to operate? Are there any zoning laws that would restrict the operation of your proposed business in the area where you intend to do business?

In addition to learning every aspect of your intended business, you should also research the potential of that particular business, particularly in the area where you plan to set up shop. For example, even though you know everything there is to know about antique furniture, there may be absolutely no market for antique furniture in your area, and as a result, your business will undoubtedly fail.

TYPE OF BUSINESS ORGANIZATION

One of the first tasks you will undertake when you decide to go into business for yourself will be selecting the type of business organization you will form. There are three basic types of business formations which are most commonly used by small businesses. They are the sole proprietorship, the partnership and the corporation. The type of business you form will affect the way in which you must operate your business, therefore, you should consider the restrictions and limitations of each before making your decision.

Nevertheless, you are not obligated to maintain a certain form of business and, if your needs change, you can change the form of your business. For example, if you start out as a sole proprietorship, but need additional funding, or someone who can contribute additional management skills, you may want to bring in a partner.

The Sole Proprietorship

The sole proprietorship is the simplest and most common business organization, and the least expensive of the three basic forms of doing business. The sole proprietorship is owned and operated by one person—the sole proprietor—and continues until his or her death or retirement. The business may be operated in the individual's personal name, or under an assumed business name, also known as a DBA (doing business as).

Generally, the business owner is required to file a business certificate with the appropriate governmental office, such as the county clerk, who determines whether that name is already in use by another business. If that occurs, then another business name must be chosen. Generally, the assumed name must not be misleading, and must not constitute unfair competition or trademark infringement. If so, the aggrieved party may petition the court to enjoin use of the name.

A sample Business Certificate is set forth in the Appendix 4.

Unlike a corporation, the sole proprietorship does not afford the owner any protection from the debts and liabilities of the business. For example, if the business incurs debts, the business creditor can go after the owner's personal assets to recover the debt. In addition, the sole proprietor has absolute authority over all business decisions, however, he or she is also personally liable for all of his or her own acts, as well as all acts of employees committed within the scope of their employment.

Taxation

The sole proprietorship itself does not pay any taxes. The sole proprietor retains the profits of the business. The income and expenses from the business are shown on IRS Schedule C, which is made part of the business owner's personal income tax returns. If Schedule C shows that the business earned a profit, that amount is added to all other income the individual earned that year from whatever source. On the other hand, if the business shows a loss, that amount is deducted, thereby reducing the total income subject to taxation. Nevertheless, a sole proprietor is required to pay self-employment tax for Social Security coverage.

The Partnership

A partnership occurs when two or more persons agree to form a business, each generally making a contribution to the venture, such as money, property or services, with the intention of sharing the profits and losses from the business. Since a corporation is a legal person, it may be a member of a partnership if such membership is in furtherance of the corporation's purpose. The partnership name may consist of the names of the partners or, as with a sole proprietorship, the partnership name may be an assumed name. Partners are responsible for the other partner's business actions, as well as their own.

The Partnership Agreement

The partners generally enter into a written partnership agreement that spells out all of the rights and responsibilities of each partner. A partnership may also arise out of an oral agreement, although such an agreement would be difficult to prove, thus a written partnership agreement is always recommended.

A well-drafted partnership agreement should include the following:

1. Type of business.
2. Amount of equity invested by each partner.
3. Division of profit or loss.
4. Partners' compensation.
5. Distribution of assets on dissolution.
6. Duration of partnership.
7. Provisions for changes or dissolving the partnership.
8. Dispute settlement clause.
9. Restrictions of authority and expenditures.

A sample partnership agreement is set forth at Appendix 5.

Taxation

Although a partnership does not pay any tax, it must file an information return setting forth the profits and losses of the partnership. The profits and losses of the partnership flow through to the individual partners. The individual partners must report their shares of the partnership profits or losses on their personal income taxes, in much the same manner as the sole proprietor. Unless the partnership agreement provides otherwise, partners generally share profits equally, and share losses in the same proportion as profits. In addition, each partner is also required to pay self-employment tax for Social Security coverage.

General and Limited Partnerships

The two basic types of partnerships are the general partnership and the limited partnership. In a general partnership, all of the partners, known as general partners, share fully in the profits, losses and management of the company. In addition, each partner has unlimited personal liability.

A limited partnership consists of one or more general partners, who manage the business and are personally liable for partnership debts, and one or more limited partners, who contribute capital and share in profits, but take no part in running the business and are not liable for the debts of the partnership beyond their capital contributions.

The advantage of a limited partnership over a general partnership is the limited liability afforded the limited partners, as long as the limited partner does not take an active role in managing the business.

The Corporation

A corporation is a legal entity, separate from its owner, created under the authority of the laws of the state in which it conducts business. This is true even if all of the shares in the corporation are owned by only one person. Control depends on stock ownership. Persons with the largest stock ownership, not the total number of shareholders, control the corporation. With control of stock shares or 51 percent of stock, a person or group is able to make policy decisions. Control is exercised through regular board of directors' meetings and annual stockholders' meetings. Records must be kept to document decisions made by the board of directors. Small, closely held corporations can operate more informally, but record-keeping cannot be eliminated entirely.

A corporation may be public or private. A public corporation is a governmental agency created by the state, such as a school district, city, town, or county.

Common usage also refers to business corporations as either public or private. A public business corporation refers to one which trades its shares to and among the general public, as opposed to a private business corporation, also known as a close corporation, whose shares are not publicly traded. This almanac is concerned with the formation of a private business corporation.

Incorporation has some advantages over the sole proprietorship and partnership forms of doing business. For example, incorporation may provide limited liability for the shareholders. Thus, if the corporation enters into a contract for the purchase of goods, and it breaches the contract and does not pay for those goods, the creditor can only enforce a judgment against the assets of the corporation. The assets of the shareholders and officers cannot be touched.

Piercing the Corporate Veil

If the shareholders do not operate the corporation as a separate and distinct entity, with all the legal formalities, a court may conclude that the business is not a true corporate entity and the court may "pierce the corporate veil." When this happens, personal liability may be imposed on the shareholders. This could occur, for example, where the shareholders commingle corporate and personal funds or do not maintain the proper corporate records. Further, officers of a corporation can be liable to stockholders for improper actions.

In addition, particularly in states where corporations are required to maintain a minimum amount of capital as a condition of doing business, courts will pierce the corporate veil if they determine that the corporation is not adequately capitalized.

There are some exceptions to the limited liability feature of incorporation. For example, creditors of closely held corporations will likely require a personal guarantee from one or more of the shareholders or officers before extending credit to the corporation. The person who gives that guarantee will be personally liable for that particular corporate debt should the corporation fail to pay.

The Corporate Name

When setting up your corporation, you must select a corporate name. This is the only name under which the corporation can legally do business. The proposed name must be cleared with the designated governmental office, such as the office of the Secretary of State. If the name you choose is the same as, or substantially similar to, that of another corporation conducting business in the state, the name will be rejected and you will have to submit another name for your corporation.

Forming the Corporation

The corporation is formed by filing a certificate of incorporation, also known as articles of incorporation, with the designated governmental office of the state, such as the office of the Secretary of State. Each state sets its own fees which must accompany the filing. The filing date of the certificate is generally the official date that the corporation is deemed to be in existence.

A sample certificate of incorporation is set forth at Appendix 6.

After the certificate is filed, there are certain formalities which must occur. Often, in small, closely held corporations, the organization meeting, first meeting of the board of directors, and first meeting of the shareholders are held on the same day, scheduled one after the other. Stock is usually issued at the organization meeting. Adoption of the corporate bylaws, which set forth basic information about the corporation, and election of the board of directors occur at the first meeting of the shareholders.

The board of directors manages the business of the corporation and establishes corporate policy. At the first meeting of the board of directors, the corporate officers are elected. The officers carry out the day-to-day business of the corporation, pursuant to the policy established by the board of directors.

The shareholders, directors, and officers may be one and the same, which is often the case in a small business. Generally, there cannot be less than three directors unless there are less than three shareholders, in which case the number of directors must at least equal the number of shareholders (e.g., one shareholder only requires one director).

Domestic and Foreign Corporations

If you incorporate in the state in which you plan to conduct all or most of your business, the corporation is known as a domestic corporation in that state, and the law of that state governs the internal affairs of the corporation. If you choose to incorporate your business in a state other than, or in addition to, the states in which you will be conducting your business, your corporation will be known as a foreign corporation in any other states in which you conduct business. In addition to the taxes and regulations of its own state of incorporation, a foreign corporation will be subject to additional taxes, fees, and regulations in the states in which it does business and is not incorporated.

Because there is no automatic right to conduct business in a state other than the state of incorporation, a corporation must first apply for authorization to do business in other states. It is best to incorporate in the state in which you will be conducting business unless, despite the additional expense, there is a good reason to incorporate elsewhere, e.g., another state's corporate law is more advantageous to your business. For example, since the state of Delaware's laws are particularly favorable towards corporations, many of the largest U.S. corporations are incorporated in Delaware. However, most of those advantages are not particularly applicable to the small business.

Corporate Taxation

The C Corporation

The standard corporation—known as a C corporation—unlike a sole proprietorship or partnership, files a corporate tax return that shows the corporation's income, which is subject to taxation by the corporation. Income received by the owner of the corporation, as a shareholder/employee, which may be in the form of salary, dividend, or interest income, is taxable to the individual and reported on his or her personal income tax returns.

When the corporation pays out salaries or interest, just as any other corporate expenses, these items are deductible, as long as the salary is reasonably related to the value of the services rendered. To avoid salaries being deemed unreasonable, you can compare them with salaries paid by other companies for similar positions.

In addition, salary payments should remain consistent. If salaries fluctuate from year to year depending on how the business is doing, the Internal Revenue Service may determine that a certain portion of the payments were actually dividends, and not salaries. This is important because dividends are subject to corporate tax, as well as taxable to the stockholder on his or her personal income tax returns, resulting in a double taxation of the same funds.

The S Corporation

In order to avoid this double tax, some corporations elect, for tax purposes, what is known as S corporation status under Subchapter S, Section 1362 of the Internal Revenue Code. An S corporation files an information return instead of a regular corporate return, and does not pay taxes on the income of the corporation. The corporate income and losses are passed through, on a pro-rata basis, to the shareholders, who report their shares of the income or losses on their personal income tax returns, much like a partnership.

In order to elect S corporation status, the corporation must meet certain statutory requirements. For example, among other requirements, an S corporation must be a domestic corporation that is not a member of an affiliated group of corporations; it cannot have more than 35 shareholders (a husband and wife may be counted as one shareholder); and the shareholders must be individuals, estates, or certain trusts, and cannot be non-resident aliens. In addition, there can only be one class of stock.

Once S corporation status is elected, it continues until revoked. Therefore, you can maintain an S corporation as long as this arrangement benefits you, assuming you continue to meet the statutory requirements.

The Professional Corporation

In most states, professionals—such as accountants, doctors, lawyers, and dentists—are permitted to form a corporation. Shareholders must be duly licensed in the profession. Many professional corporations are formed to allow the shareholders to take advantage of the tax benefits of incorporation. The shareholders of a professional corporation also enjoy limited liability for all claims except in the case of professional malpractice. If a shareholder commits an act of professional malpractice, he or she is personally liable.

Section 1244 Stock

If stock issued by a corporation meets certain legal requirements set forth in Section 1244 of the Internal Revenue Code, the Board of Directors may designate stock as Section 1244 stock. The advantage of Section 1244 stock is that it allows the shareholder to claim any losses on his or her stock investment, up to a specified maximum—presently $50,000— as an ordinary loss instead of a capital loss.

The distinction between ordinary and capital loss is that ordinary losses are fully deductible from ordinary income whereas capital losses, while fully deductible from capital gains, if any, are only partially deductible from ordinary income—the present statutory limit being $3,000.

A sample Section 1244 Stock Resolution is set forth at Appendix 7.

The Limited Liability Company

The Limited Liability Company (LLC) is a new form of business organization which is gaining attention throughout the country. The LLC has features of both a partnership and a corporation. For tax purposes, it is treated like a partnership. The profits and losses of the business are distributed to the owners and investors, and reported on their personal income tax returns. However, the LLC has the added advantage of the limited personal liability enjoyed by the corporation. This is a particularly attractive feature for the small business owner, who may be concerned about the unlimited liability of a sole proprietorship. In fact, this threat of personal exposure deters many potential entrepreneurs from starting new businesses.

Although the present S corporation operates in much the same way as an LLC—i.e., it limits personal liability and is taxed like a partnership—the S corporation is much more complex and subject to many more restrictions than the LLC. For example, whereas the S corporation limits membership to individuals, estates and certain trusts, which can total no more than 35, the LLC is more flexible, allowing corporations, partnerships, charitable organizations, pension plans, nonresident aliens and other trusts to participate. In addition, the LLC may offer more than just one class of stock, unlike the S corporation.

The other two forms of business organization that protect personal assets from exposure—the regular corporation and the limited partnership—each have their drawbacks. As discussed above, the regular corporation involves double taxation of dividend income, and the limited partnership runs the risk of reclassification as a general partnership if the limited partner is determined to have taken an active part in managing the business.

Nevertheless, the LLC is not for everyone. The LLC restricts the transferability of stock and other company interests, whereas the corporation allows unrestricted transfer. Thus, if your business will require the right to transfer interests without restriction, the LLC is not the right choice. In any event, since laws concerning the LLC vary from state to state, until a uniform LLC law is adopted by all jurisdictions, it is imperative that you thoroughly investigate the LLC regulations for the states in which you intend to do business before deciding on using this form of organization.

CHOOSING THE BUSINESS LOCATION

The appropriate amount of time and research should be spent in choosing the proper location for your business. The location of your business is a major factor in its success or failure. The proper choice of a location for your business is governed by, among other things, the type of business you operate.

For example, if your business is a retail clothing store, you don't want it to be located in an industrial district unless you are counting on doing all of your business with factory workers on their lunch breaks. If you operate a pharmacy, you may want to choose a location near a hospital or medical group. It would be advantageous for an automobile insurance company to open shop across from the Department of Motor Vehicles.

If you plan to lease space in a shopping mall, you should investigate the competition, and make sure that the traffic patterns in the mall are advantageous to your location. You would ideally like to be located next to stores that will generate traffic for your store. For example, it may be favorable to locate a toy store next to a children's clothing store.

In addition, consider the types of services your business may require in its own operation. Locating near such businesses will reduce your own company's costs. An international shipping company may need to be located in close proximity to an airport, to avoid the expense of transporting shipments long distances and to expedite deliveries. Similarly, a law firm specializing in criminal law may want to be located near the criminal court to reduce travel time and costs.

Researching the Marketplace

Before you commit to a certain location, you must do some research into the sales potential of that area, including the population and demographics. You should be able to obtain such information from the local government office. To illustrate, if you plan to open a dry cleaning service in a small town, you can use population and demographic statistics to make a ballpark estimate of the potential number of users of dry cleaning services in the area. You must then take into consideration the number of dry cleaners already operating in the town and consider the length of time they have been operating. A local dry cleaner who has been in business for 20 years, serving the same community, probably has a very loyal client base.

If your research shows that the total number of potential customers is small and that there are a number of long-standing businesses in the area similar to your intended business, your chances of succeeding in that location are slim, unless you can offer additional services. For example, you may consider supplementing your dry cleaning service with shoe repair, offering a pick-up and delivery service, or operating during nontraditional hours, if those services are not already available in the area.

In addition, you should consider whether the area will be experiencing any population growth in the near future. You may be able to get some helpful information from the local zoning commission. Investigate whether there are any plans to build additional housing developments in the community. If so, then you may be able to claim a number of newcomers to the area as your customers.

You should also make sure that the economics of the area are in line with the business you wish to open. An expensive designer boutique will not fare well in a low income neighborhood.

Whether you are buying an existing business, or starting a new business, make sure that there are no impending changes in the area which will adversely affect your business. For example, if you plan to operate a diner near a factory in order to attract the lunchtime crowd, make sure that there are no plans for that factory to close down, leaving you without customers.

Leasing Commercial Space

After you have determined the appropriate location for your business, you must negotiate an affordable lease for that space. Some important considerations include the term of the lease, the right to renew the lease, and the monthly rent and required security deposit. Since start-up businesses are statistically risky, landlords may require advance payment of up to six months rent as security.

In addition, you should make sure that the services you are entitled to are included in the lease, such as heat, electricity, and air conditioning, and how their cost to you is computed. If your business is the type that invites customers, you must make sure that there is adequate parking, for both the customers and the employees, and that there are restroom facilities available. Generally, commercial space is leased on a price per square foot of rentable area basis. Determine the prevailing rates for similar space in buildings in the same general area, in order to establish a basis for negotiating the best rates for your space.

A sample commercial lease agreement is set forth at Appendix 8.

Office Layout

At the center of all businesses, there is usually a general office that oversees the operations of the business. The general office may be one small room, or it may occupy an entire building floor, depending on the size and nature of the business. Activities of the business are usually planned and coordinated in, and directives issued from, the general office, Management is usually located in the general office. Office personnel usually carry out such tasks as accounting, billing and payroll. Business records are also maintained and located in the general office.

In order to make sure the general office is run as efficiently as possible, there are certain basic requirements which should be met, such as adequate lighting, desk space and phone lines. In addition, office space should be designed for easier coordination of tasks. Employees performing similar or related tasks, such as salespersons, should be located in the same area. A space designer should be engaged to render advice on the various configurations that will best suit your needs and make efficient use out of the space.

Subletting Space

It would be advantageous for you to negotiate the right to sublet all or a portion of your space, particularly if you enter into a long-term lease. For example, your business may flourish and you may require a larger space much sooner than anticipated. On the other hand, you may determine that a large portion of the space you are leasing is unused. In either scenario, it would be beneficial to be able to sublet all or part of your leased space. The subtenants would have to abide by the same lease provisions you do. You must also negotiate how profits from subleasing, if any, will be distributed.

A sample sublease agreement is set forth at Appendix 9.

The Home-Based Business

According to the Small Business Administration, the number of people who operate their businesses out of their homes is on the rise. It may come as quite a surprise to many entrepreneurs, that operating a home-based business may, in fact, be illegal under the zoning laws of many jurisdictions. In fact, statutes banning home-based businesses are rarely enforced unless the business creates problems, such as excessive noise, which cause complaints to be made. The ban on home-based businesses stems from antiquated laws concerned with the effects of dangerous or obtrusive businesses—e.g., factories in residential communities. Of course, those laws could not have contemplated the types of home-based businesses prevalent in the computer age, such as desktop publishing companies.

Before you begin your home-based business, find out how your property is zoned. If you live in an area designated as residential, as opposed to agricultural, commercial, or industrial, you must determine whether there are any restrictions or prohibitions on home-based businesses in the zoning regulations. If there are restrictions, try to adapt your business to comply with them, if at all possible. If home-based businesses are prohibited, however, you must apply for a variance or permit to operate the business.

CHAPTER 4:
MARKETING THE BUSINESS

IN GENERAL

The goal of every business is to make a profit on the sale of its product or service to the public. In order to do so, the public has to be made aware of the existence of that product or service. You can have the best product in the world, but if nobody knows it exists, you won't earn a dime. Exposing your product is accomplished through a process known as marketing. Business growth will be influenced by how well the small business owner can plan and execute a marketing program.

Marketing involves the promotion and advertising of your product or service to existing and prospective buyers and users. In order to reach and capture the largest and most profitable share of your potential market, a comprehensive marketing plan should be prepared.

Marketing is the small business owner's most important organizing tool. There are four basic aspects of marketing, often called the "four P's":

1. Product: The item or service you sell.

2. Price: The amount you charge for your product or service.

3. Promote: The ways you inform your market as to who, what and where you are.

4. Provide: The channels you use to take the product to the customer.

DEFINING YOUR MARKET

Marketing encompasses much more than just advertising or selling. For example, a major part of marketing involves researching your customer base. You should define your target audience; their financial capabilities; and their needs and desires. You must determine a customer profile and the geographic size of the market. This is the general market potential. Knowing the number and strength of your competitors, and then estimating the share of business you will take from them, will give you the market potential specific to your enterprise.

The first step is to determine who will be the primary purchasers and users of your product or service—i.e., your market. Your analysis should include people who already need and use your specific product or service, as well as potential customers. You should analyze that group even further, breaking it down into smaller market segments, so that you can determine which particular group is most profitable for you and to whom most of your efforts should be directed.

For example, your hair salon may have a primarily female market. It would be difficult and cost prohibitive to market your hair salon to all females; therefore, you must narrow your market down to your most favorable customer base. Your first step in this process would be to conduct a market analysis by categorizing and identifying your customers according to like characteristics, such as age.

The results may indicate that your customer base is 20% under 25, 20% over 45, and that 60% of your customers fall into the 25 to 45 range. Thus, it will be the market consisting of females between the ages of 25 to 45 to whom you will most aggressively promote and advertise your hair salon services.

You can break your market segment down even further by comparing other available data, such as income level and profession. You may thus discover that your most profitable market segment consists of career women aged 25 to 45 who earn over $60,000 per year. You can use this information to direct your marketing efforts at the clientele who will earn you the most profit.

MARKET PENETRATION

Once you have defined your most profitable market, you must then determine how to capture the largest portion of that group. In the example of the hair salon discussed above, efforts to penetrate the market might include mailing flyers to the homes and offices of women who fit the profile and advertising in publications that would most likely include that demographic group in their readership. You may also be able to get some free advertising by sending press releases concerning your new business to the local newspapers.

Another approach is to ask your existing customers for referrals, as it is likely that they have friends and co-workers who fall in the same general category. Think of additional services you can offer that might appeal to your specific market, such as lunch-time or after-work specials for the career woman customer.

Use your own personal experience to think like the customer and to determine what products or services would attract the most people. Distribute free samples. Employ questionnaires to find out your customers' thoughts, opinions, and needs. Use this information to determine what they liked or disliked about your product or service—e.g., packaging, efficiency, etc. Try to accommodate their suggestions wherever possible, particularly when there is a consensus about a particular idea.

Promotional items on which your company logo and telephone number are imprinted may be effective marketing tools. These items serve to establish name recognition and easy access. The more useful the item the better, since junk items would likely be thrown in the garbage. Popular promotional items include memo pads, pens, refrigerator magnets, key chains, and shopping bags.

THE COMPETITION

You should have already determined the number of similar businesses in your area before you established your location. Depending on the type of business you operate, carefully examine your competition. If you are an inventor, and have proposed a new product, do the research necessary to make sure that there aren't 15 different versions of your product already in existence.

If you operate a service business or a retail store, visit a competitor's establishment, sample the product or service, and observe the staff. Try and determine who your competitor's customers are and what satisfies them. Determine whether your competitor offers any additional services that you have overlooked, such as credit, free delivery, or convenient parking facilities. Analyze their advertisements.

Consider whether your prices are competitive. Sometimes, price will be the only difference between you and your competitor, where products or services are substantially similar.

You must give the customers what they want or they will go elsewhere. In that connection, determine what your competitors are not doing that you can do, or what they are doing that you can do better, to attract additional customers. If they have a particular marketing scheme that appears to be working, learn from it and adapt it for your own business.

REVIEW YOUR MARKETING PLAN REGULARLY

You must set goals for your company, both long and short-term. In this way, you will be able to see if you are progressing, regressing, or stagnating. Regularly review your marketing plan to see if it is working or if it needs to be modified. Determine whether your customer base is expanding and if you are earning profits.

Keep tabs on your competitors, and find out if any new, similar operations have opened up shop in your vicinity. Keep abreast of any new developments or trends that affect your business that may increase sales and profits. A great deal of helpful information and advice can be gathered by contacting your trade association.

CHAPTER 5:
FINANCING THE BUSINESS

IN GENERAL

One of the most important aspects of operating a business is maintaining adequate cash flow. One of the leading causes of business failure is insufficient start-up capital. If the business takes off, more money will be needed to carry the increased operational costs, which may include additional inventory and payroll, as well as expansion funds. Basically, you should have enough money to cover the operating expenses of your company for at least one year, including your salary.

Many small business owners use their own money to start their new businesses. Overall, small firms rely more on owner capital and less on external debt capital than larger firms. In addition, small firms are more dependent than large firms on short-term debt relative to long-term debt. Most small firms use external financing only occasionally. Less than half of small firms borrow once or more during a year. However, small firms experiencing rapid growth or those with high volumes of receivables require frequent external financing. Thus, unless personal funds are unlimited, you will have to look to outside financing at some point to keep the business afloat.

Of course, your ability to acquire outside financing depends heavily on whether you are starting the business from scratch or if you are buying an existing business. An existing business will usually have a track record, in which case a lender will be more likely to risk funds, whereas a new business poses a much greater risk. Risking your own funds is an indicator to outside investors of how serious and committed you are about your business.

Most small firms have used some form of financing. According to the Small Business Administration, of all small firms, 61 percent had used trade credit and 56 percent had used a traditional financing source such as a credit line, mortgage loan, or lease. In 1993, 26 percent had lines of credit, 9 percent had financial leases, 6 percent had mortgage loans, 14 percent had equipment loans, and 24 percent had motor vehicle loans.

The credit card is also a very important financing source: 39 percent of small firms used personal credit cards for business purposes and 28 percent used business credit cards in 1993. About 40 percent of firms with fewer than 10 employees used personal credit cards compared with 22-24 percent of larger firms with 50 or more employees. In 1998, an estimated 45-50 percent of small firms used credit cards.

The cost of borrowed funds is higher for small firms. Interest rates on bank loans for small firms average 2 or 3 percentage points more than the prime rate. Fixed-rate loans are usually more expensive than floating-rate loans.

RAISING CAPITAL

The capital you are seeking to raise will likely be a combination of debt capital and equity capital. Debt capital is the money you raise through loans which are repaid with interest, usually through a bank. Equity capital is the money you raise by giving up some portion of ownership in your business, such as through the sale of stock or a partnership arrangement.

There should be a balance between your debt and equity capital, since too much of either can be bad. If you incur too much debt capital, your company will look unstable, and it is unlikely you will be able to obtain any more financing should the need arise. If you raise too much equity capital, you run the risk of losing control of your business to the investors, who generally require a provision allowing them to replace you if they suspect that you are unable to adequately manage the business. In addition to the assistance provided by the SBA, as discussed below, common sources of debt and equity capital include those described below.

DEBT CAPITAL

Bank Loans

Access to credit is vital for small business survival, and a key supplier of credit to small firms is the commercial banking system. Approximately 67 percent of all small firms that borrow from traditional sources obtain their money from commercial banks, followed by finance companies, the second most prominent lender to small business. Of the small firms that borrow from traditional credit sources, the following companies obtain their financing from commercial banks:

1. 59 percent of firms with 0 employees,

2. 64 percent of firms with 1–4 employees,

3. 68 percent of firms with 5-9 employees,

4. 73 percent of firms with 10–19 employees,

5. 84 percent of firms with 20-99 employees,

6. 86 percent of firms with 100–499 employees.

In June 1999, commercial banks had $1.1 trillion in business loans outstanding (commercial and industrial and commercial mortgage loans), of which 35 percent—$398 billion—was in small business loans of less than $1 million. The growth in small business loans is estimated to be approximately 3.0 percent for loans under $100,000, 8.1 percent for loans of $100,000 to $250,000, and 7.7 percent for loans of $250,000 to $1 million.

The number of small business loans increased considerably, from 7.9 million in 1997 to 9.2 million in 1998. However, almost all of the increase (19.3 percent) came in the smallest loan category, those under $100,000. Many of these loans reflect promotions by larger banks of business credit cards and small lines of credit. The other size categories of small loans had a less than 2 percent increase.

Thus, it is critical to the health and growth of a small business to know which banks are meeting the credit needs of small firms.

A List of the Top 55 Commercial Banks Providing Loans to Small Businesses is set forth at Appendix 10.

Because banks operate on a relatively low profit margin, they are not in the practice of taking risks. A bank is much more likely to lend money to a successful business which does not need financing to keep the business running, but is seeking funds to expand its operations. Banks often require a guaranty of payment from the principal shareholders or officers of the company. Thus, if the company defaults in its repayment of credit, the lender can go after the personal assets of the individual guarantors.

The approval of a loan—short-term or long-term—generally requires that the business be in good financial standing and that the business offer collateral to secure the loan. There are certain steps you can take in preparing your loan package that may increase your chances of securing financing. You should emphasize your experience and track record in the particular business.

The Business Plan

The first step in successfully obtaining a loan for your small business is to prepare a comprehensive business plan, which should precisely describe your business, including your product or service, key employees of the company, the market, the costs, potential profit, etc. The new business owner will have to demonstrate to the lender or investor the potential of the new business in order to obtain funding. A well developed business plan is essential in this regard and is a crucial part of any loan package.

The purpose of your business plan is to precisely define your business, its goals, and its potential. It should show your company in the best possible light, without being misleading, and without divulging too much information should a competitor get his or her hands on it. A properly drawn business plan should include as its basic components your company's balance sheets, income statements, and cash flow analyses.

Before you begin formulating your business plan, there are certain steps you should follow:

1. Research your proposed business in detail, including the market, the competition, the sales and profit potential and the amount of start-up money you will need for your particular type of business;

2. Research the location where you will establish your business to make sure it is appropriate for the type of business you are proposing—location can make or break a new business.

3. Gather complete business records, including all financial data which relates to your business; and

4. Define your goals and objectives.

A well-organized business plan should include the following components:

Introduction

The introduction should give a detailed description of the business and its goals and discuss the ownership of the business and the legal structure. You should also list the skills and experience you bring to the business and the advantages your business has over its competition.

Marketing

The section on marketing should discuss the product and/or service offered; identify the customer demand for the product and/or service; and identify the market, its size and locations. You should also explain how your product and/or service will be advertised and marketed and explain the pricing strategy.

Financial Management

The section on financial management should explain your source and the amount of initial equity capital. It should set forth a monthly operating budget and an expected return on investment and monthly cash flow for the first year. You should provide projected income statements and balance sheets for a two-year period and discuss your break-even point. You should also explain your personal balance sheet and method of compensation. Discuss who will maintain your accounting records and how they will be kept and address alternative approaches to any problem that may develop.

Operations

The operations section should explain how the business will be managed on a day-to-day basis and discuss hiring and personnel procedures. Insurance, lease or rental agreements, and issues pertinent to your business should be discussed. Explain the equipment necessary to produce the products or services offered by the business, and account for production and delivery of products and services.

Concluding Statement

The concluding statement should summarize your business goals and objectives and express your commitment to the success of your business.

A sample business plan format is set forth at Appendix 11.

Financial Statement

In addition to your business plan, you must generally provide the loan officer with projected cash flow for the first three years of business, a list of collateral available to secure the loan, and a financial statement of your own resources and expenses.

A sample financial statement is set forth at Appendix 12.

Repayment of the loan generally is made in installments at various intervals e.g., monthly, quarterly, etc., depending on the duration of the loan. The short-term loan—one maturing in 60 to 90 days—is particularly helpful for the seasonal business.

Banks may also offer what are known as accounts receivable loans, whereby the bank lends on a percentage, e.g. 80%, of the company's outstanding invoices on a short-term basis. The invoice payments are forwarded to the bank, which deducts the loan amount plus interest and forwards the balance to the company. In some cases, the bank will act as a "factor," in which case you actually sell your accounts receivable to the bank, which assumes collection if the customers default in payment.

The SBA 7(a) Loan Guaranty Program

The 7(a) Loan Guaranty Program is the SBA's primary loan program. The SBA reduces risk to lenders by guaranteeing major portions of loans made to small businesses. This enables the lenders to provide financing to small businesses when funding is otherwise unavailable on reasonable terms. The eligibility requirements and credit criteria of the program are very broad in order to accommodate a wide range of financing needs.

When a small business applies to a lending institution for a loan, the lender reviews the application and decides if it merits a loan on its own or if it requires additional support in the form of an SBA guaranty. SBA backing on the loan is then requested by the lender. In guaranteeing the loan, the SBA assures the lender that, in the event the borrower does not repay the loan, the government will reimburse the lending institution for a portion of its loss. By providing this guaranty, the SBA is able to help tens of thousands of small businesses every year get financing they would not otherwise obtain.

To qualify for an SBA guaranty, a small business must meet the 7(a) criteria, and the lender must certify that it could not provide funding on reasonable terms except with an SBA guaranty. The SBA can then guarantee as much as 80 percent on loans of up to $100,000 and 75 percent on loans of more than $100,000. In most cases, the maximum guaranty is $750,000 (75 percent of $1 million).

Processing the Loan

The small business owner must submit a loan application to a lender for initial review. If the lender approves the loan subject to an SBA guaranty, a copy of the application and a credit analysis are forwarded by the lender to the nearest SBA office.

A sample Application for Business Loan (SBA Form 4) is set forth at Appendix 13.

After SBA approval, the lending institution closes the loan and disburses the funds. You make monthly loan payments directly to the lender. As with any loan, you are responsible for repaying the full amount of the loan. There are no balloon payments, prepayment penalties, application fees or points permitted with 7(a) loans. Repayment plans may be tailored to each business.

Use of Proceeds

Proceeds from an SBA 7(a) loan may be used to expand or renovate facilities; purchase machinery, equipment, fixtures and leasehold improvements; finance receivables and augment working capital; refinance existing debt with compelling reason; finance seasonal lines of credit; construct commercial buildings; and/or purchase land or buildings.

Terms, Interest Rates and Fees

The length of time for repayment depends on the use of the proceeds and the ability of your business to repay—usually five to 10 years for working capital, and up to 25 years for fixed assets such as the purchase or major renovation of real estate or purchase of equipment (not to exceed the useful life of the equipment).

Both fixed and variable interest rates are available. Rates are pegged at no more than 2.25 percent over the lowest prime rate for loans with maturities of less than seven years and up to 2.75 percent for seven years or longer. For loans under $50,000, rates may be slightly higher.

The SBA charges the lender a nominal fee to provide a guaranty, and the lender may pass this charge on to the applicant. The fee is based on the maturity of the loan and the dollar amount that the SBA guarantees. On any loan with a maturity of one year or less, the fee is just one-quarter percent of the guaranteed portion of the loan. On loans with maturities of more than one year where the portion that the SBA guarantees is $80,000 or less, the guaranty fee is 2 percent of the guaranteed portion. On loans with maturities of more than one year, where the SBA's portion exceeds $80,000, the guaranty fee is figured on an incremental scale, beginning at 3 percent.

Collateral

The applicant must pledge sufficient assets, to the extent that they are reasonably available, to adequately secure the loan. Personal guaranties are required from all the principal owners of the business. Liens on personal assets of the principals may be required. However, in most cases a loan will not be declined where insufficient collateral is the only unfavorable factor.

Eligibility

A small business generally must be operated for profit and fall within the size standards set by the SBA in order to be eligible for a 7(a) loan. The SBA determines if the business qualifies as a small business based on the average number of employees during the preceding 12 months or on sales averaged over the previous three years. Loans cannot be made to businesses engaged in speculation or investment.

The maximum size standards of the business are as follows:

1. Manufacturing—from 500 to 1,500 employees

2. Wholesaling—100 employees Services—from $2.5 million to $21.5 million in annual receipts

3. Retailing—from $5 million to $21 million

4. General construction—from $13.5 million to $17 million

5. Special trade construction—average annual receipts not to exceed $7 million

6. Agriculture—from $0.5 million to $9 million

Line of Credit

A line of credit extended to a company by a bank operates in much the same way as a personal credit card. The lender will generally conduct a credit check before establishing a maximum credit line, which the company can draw upon as needed.

Trade Credit

Delaying payment to suppliers for merchandise received is a form of short-term loan. Suppliers often encourage early payment by discounting invoices which are paid within a certain specified time, e.g., 30 days. On the other hand, payments which are delayed beyond a specified time, e.g., 60 days, will usually incur interest.

Equipment Loans and Leases

When financing is needed to purchase the company's equipment, the equipment itself may serve as collateral for a loan. Alternatively, the company may enter into a leasing agreement whereby the leasing company holds title to the equipment for the duration of the lease, which generally extends for the designated life of the equipment. The company makes payments during the lease period, which in the aggregate will have exceeded the purchase price of the equipment by the end of the lease term. Depending on the lease provisions, at the end of the lease, the company may be able to take title to the equipment for a nominal sum.

EQUITY CAPITAL

Small Business Investment Companies

Under the Small Business Investment Act, the SBA licenses privately owned small business investment companies (SBICs) which provide funds to eligible small businesses. The SBIC generally raises its investment funds by borrowing from the federal government or banks.

Like the SBA, the SBIC also requires that the small business be unable to raise money through other channels. Although SBICs are more willing to take risks on new businesses, they are profit-motivated organizations and, thus, will closely examine the profit potential of your business.

Venture Capital Companies

Another source of funding for small businesses—usually on a short-term basis—is a venture capital company. Venture capital companies are in the business of taking risks in return for larger returns and, thus they will generally want to take an active role in your business. You may obtain information on venture capital from the SBA, as well as from your investment adviser, banker, lawyer and accountant.

Individual Investors

You may be able to raise money by bringing in investors with whom you will share the profits, if any, from your business. Such investors can be known individuals, such as relatives, friends and business associates, and may also include unknown investors, such as ex-entrepreneurs and wealthy business people, who have money to invest. Like venture capital companies, private investors often desire to take an active control in the business.

PURCHASING AN EXISTING SMALL BUSINESS

If you purchase an existing small business, it is prudent to engage an attorney to handle the transaction. Your attorney will generally enlist other professionals, including a business appraiser, an accountant, a banker, an insurance representative, etc., to assist in finalizing the transaction. The business appraiser and the accountant may be the same person if he or she possesses the requisite experience and training necessary to properly evaluate a business.

The transaction will generally begin with an evaluation of all of the economic aspects of the business. A thorough evaluation, conducted by an experienced business appraiser, will assist the buyer in making an informed decision concerning his or her potential success in operating the particular business. The evaluation also assists the seller in setting a fair and realistic purchase price for the business.

The buyer should consider such factors as his or her experience in the field; the demand for the product or service offered by the business; the failure rate of similar businesses; the existence of competitive businesses; particularly those located in the same area; the cost of operation; and the buyer's ability to keep afloat until the business starts to turn a profit.

An accountant may also be hired to thoroughly investigate the company's financial condition. Generally, the accountant will review the company's financial statements and tax returns, and report on the overall profits and losses of the business and the tax considerations. Based on the accountant's review, the buyer will be able to determine any potential financial problems and the likelihood that the business will succeed.

The attorney will review all of the organizational documents of the business. Depending on the type of business you are purchasing (e.g., corporation or partnership), such documents may include the partnership agreement, certificate of incorporation and bylaws, and any related documents. In addition, the attorney will review the deed and title, and related documents, to confirm ownership and ascertain any potential problems or limitations on the transfer.

Other important aspects of the business which the attorney will review and investigate may include: the lease and zoning regulations, particularly if the location of the business is a primary asset; the legal department files to ascertain the existence of any pending or potential lawsuits; the proper registration of the business name and any trademarks; personnel matters, including the existence of employment contracts, retirement plans, union agreements, etc.; and any other information useful in determining the viability of the business.

Be particularly aware of any potential problems that will affect the location of the business, particularly if the seller appears anxious to finalize the transaction. For example, if you are considering the purchase of a profitable diner which has the lunchtime crowd of the local factory as its main customer base, make sure that the factory has not made any plans to close its doors. Many businesses are sold while they are still showing a profit after the owner discovers an impending change in the area which will adversely affect the business.

After a value has been placed on the business, the parties negotiate the terms of the deal. The attorney for one of the parties will then prepare an agreement to purchase the business, which is reviewed by all parties and finalized after all of the points have been discussed and agreed upon. Once the agreement is finalized, it will be executed by the parties to the sale, and the buyer will obtain the financing necessary to complete the sale. The final step in the transfer of a business is the closing, when the purchaser pays the agreed upon purchase price and receives the transfer documents and business records.

In searching for your ideal business opportunity, you may confront individuals who will encourage you to participate in a particular type of business venture, generally requiring you to make an initial investment or a pay a substantial fee. The types of business ventures which may be offered include franchises and distributorships.

Although some of these business opportunities may be legitimate, many are not. Their lure is usually a promise of huge profits, guaranteed sales, and extensive company support. Unfortunately, their only "business" is to take your money and run. When confronted with such an opportunity, you must investigate all aspects of the business venture offered, and the company offering it, before you hand over any money or sign any contracts. If the company is not legitimate, you will probably not be able to get your money back by the time you discover the fraud.

There are certain preliminary warning signs which should alert you to the possibility of a business opportunity fraud scheme. For example, if the individual is reluctant to put the terms of the offer down in writing, that is a cause for concern. If you are being rushed into making the deal, and discouraged from seeking legal advice, you should be wary. You may be told that the offer will only be available for a very short period. Resist such pressure tactics, and seek professional advice.

You should ask to see all pertinent company documents, such as the company's track record, including its financial statements for the past several years and a list of the officers and directors of the company. You should also request references, particularly from other investors. Make your own inquiries. Call the Better Business Bureau, and consult your banker and investment advisor.

If you do invest in a business venture and find that the company's promises to you are not being fulfilled and that you cannot get any cooperation, contact your local law enforcement authorities and complain. Even if it is too late for you to recover your investment, you will assist in protecting others from being victimized by the same individuals.

CHAPTER 6:
EMPLOYER/EMPLOYEE RELATIONS

HIRING EMPLOYEES

Managing an efficient, competent staff of employees is crucial to the success of your business. Thus, the hiring of employees should be carried out very carefully. You must look at your business from beginning to end, and consider what tasks must be carried out to accomplish its purpose. Largely depending upon the nature of your business, you must determine the number of employees you need and the responsibilities you want those employees to undertake.

Determining the number of employees you need to operate your business efficiently can be difficult and often cannot be predicted until you have been in business for awhile. Of course, depending on the type of business you operate, it may be easier to determine the number of employees needed in certain departments. For example, if you operate a clothing manufacturing business, and you have ten sewing machines, you will need ten employees to operate those machines. You may want to have one or two back-up employees who perform other tasks, but who can also operate the machine when the regular operator is out sick or on vacation.

Determining the number of employees you need also depends on the efficiency of a particular employee. Some employees have the ability to do the work of two or three standard employees. On the other hand, two less able employees may only be able to accomplish as much as one standard employee. If you find an employee who turns out to be particularly valuable to the Company, you may wish to enter into an employment agreement with him or her.

A sample employment agreement is set forth at Appendix 14.

Before you begin hiring, refer to the organizational chart included in your business plan to determine what tasks each department of your company will undertake. You can then determine the smallest number of employees you believe you need to accomplish all of those tasks, and prepare a realistic job description for each employee in each department. You should also prepare a qualifications sheet listing the requirements of each particular position, such as level of education and experience. This will at least give you a starting point. It is far easier, and more economical, to hire additional employees as needed than to fire existing employees, and risk exposure to legal claims, however unsubstantiated their claims may be.

Employee Handbook

You should consider preparing an employee handbook detailing the written policies and procedures of the company which each employee is expected to follow. Items that can be covered in the employee handbook may include company dress code, vacation, holiday and sick leave policies, employee benefits, company hours, company policy concerning performance evaluations and salary increases, and disciplinary procedures. This handbook is quite important, as it puts the employee on notice as to what behaviors are expected and what behaviors will not be tolerated.

Employee Polygraph Protection Act

When interviewing a prospective employee, one trait an employer looks for is honesty. Of course, this trait is not often readily apparent during a 15-minute job interview. Employers might wish to conduct a lie detector test of every employee. However, under the Employee Polygraph Protection Act (the Act), most private employers are prohibited from using lie detector tests either for hiring employees or for existing employees.

There are certain exemptions to the Act. For example, the federal, state, and local governments are not subject to the law. In addition, private employers who are engaged in the manufacture, distribution, or dispensing of pharmaceuticals, and security services, such as security guard services, are permitted to administer lie detector tests to certain prospective employees, subject to restrictions. There are also situations in which the Act permits testing of persons suspected of employee theft that resulted in economic loss to the employer, also subject to restrictions.

In those situations where lie detector tests are legally permitted, the employee has certain rights relating to the length and conduct of the test. In addition, the employer is required to give the employee advance written notice. An employee may refuse to take the test or may request to discontinue taking the test during its administration. The results of an employee's lie detector test are private and are not permitted to be disclosed to any unauthorized person.

Violations of the Act may result in civil penalties up to $10,000. Such a legal action may be brought by a job applicant, an employee, or by the Secretary of Labor. In addition, where a specific state law or collective bargaining agreement provides for a more restrictive ban on lie detector tests, the federal government defers to that law.

Federal Immigration Reform and Control Act

The federal Immigration Reform and Control Act of 1990 (IRCA) is a mechanism by which illegal immigration is controlled through the employment system. The IRCA, which is governed by the United States Immigration and Naturalization Service, requires public and private employers to determine that each person hired is legally authorized to work. The IRCA is comprised of two parts—the anti-discrimination provision and the employer sanction provision.

The anti-discrimination provision prohibits employment discrimination based on national origin and citizenship status and requires that employers treat all job applicants equally. Employers who violate this provision, or retaliate against employees who file discrimination charges, are subject to monetary sanctions ranging up to $2,000 per individual for the first offense, up to $5,000 per individual for the second offense, and up to $10,000 per individual for subsequent offenses.

The employer sanction provision is concerned with the hiring of undocumented workers. Under this provision, employers must complete IRS Form I-9, which is used to verify the employment eligibility and identity of employees. The I-9 form must be completed and retained by the employer for any employees hired after November 6, 1986. The employer must file the I-9 form within three days from the hiring date.

A sample INS Employment Eligibility Verification Form (INS Form I-9) is set forth at Appendix 15.

In order to complete the form, the employer must review documentation provided by the employee which satisfies the employment eligibility and identity requirement. The employer cannot request a particular form of identification. Rather, the employee is free to choose from any of the forms of identification acceptable to the INS.

A list of forms of identification that can be used to satisfy the requirements of the IRCA is set forth at Appendix 16.

Individuals who were employed prior to November 6, 1986 are not subject to the IRCA, and the employer cannot be penalized for retaining those employees, even if they are illegal aliens. However, if any documents provided to the employer are time-dated, employment eligibility should be reverified.

The IRCA imposes the same monetary sanctions against employers who violate the employer sanction provision as those who violate the anti-discrimination provision. In addition, an employer who does not file the I-9 form is also subject to penalties ranging up to $1,000 per employee.

INDEPENDENT CONTRACTORS

During the course of your business, you may engage individuals to perform certain tasks as independent contractors. An independent contractor is generally defined as a person who contracts with another to perform services for that person, but who is not controlled by the other nor subject to the other's right to control with respect to physical conduct in the performance of the undertaking.

A sample independent contractor agreement is set forth at Appendix 17.

An independent contractor is not an employee. Therefore, the business owner does not have to withhold tax from the independent contractor's checks, nor does the employer have to contribute to Social Security or unemployment tax on behalf of the independent contractor.

At times, the IRS may attempt to reclassify independent contractors as employees. This can be very costly to the employer, in that the employer would then be liable for withholding tax, Social Security contributions, and unemployment tax withholding, as well as penalties and interest on those amounts due.

To determine whether or not an individual is likely to be reclassified by the IRS from independent contractor status to employee status, courts have established 20 common law factors which must be taken into account. The factors that may indicate employee status are the following:

1. If the worker is required to comply with the employer's instruction as to when, where, and how he is to work.

2. If the employer trains the worker to perform in a particular manner.

3. If the employer requires the worker to render personal service.

4. If the employer hires, supervises, and pays the worker's staff.

5. If the employer and the worker have a continuing relationship.

6. If the worker is required to work during hours set by the employer.

7. If the worker is required to work full-time for the employer.

8. If the worker performs the work on the employer's premises, particularly if the work could be performed elsewhere.

9. If the employer requires the worker to perform services in a particular order or sequence.

10. If the worker is required to submit oral or written reports to the employer.

11. If payment is made by the hour, week, or month as opposed to a per job basis.

12. If the employer pays the worker's business or traveling expenses.

13. If the employer furnishes the tools and materials to the worker.

14. If there is a lack of investment by the worker in the facilities required to perform services and dependence on the employer for such facilities.

15. If the worker realizes no profit or loss as a result of the services rendered.

16. If the worker works exclusively for the employer.

17. If the worker does not make his or her services available to the general public.

18. If the employer maintains the right to discharge the worker, which would not be possible of the individual were an independent contractor working under a contract.

19. If the worker has the right to end the relationship with the employer without continuing to render services. An independent contractor would be bound by the contract to finish the job.

20. If the worker's services are integral to the business operations.

In addition to the above criteria, Section 530 of the Revenue Act of 1978 serves as a "safe harbor" for employers who treated individuals as independent contractors for federal employment tax purposes, even if they were in error, as long as the employer had a reasonable basis for doing so.

SETTING EMPLOYEE SALARIES

Some factors which should be considered in establishing appropriate salaries include the level of skill required for the particular position, the importance of the position to the company, the geographic location of your business, and the rate of pay for similar positions with other companies.

Of course, the more valuable an employee is to the company, the higher salary that employee deserves. There is no such thing as a governmentally set "maximum" wage thus this figure may be agreed upon entirely between you and your prospective employee. However, as explained more fully below, there are federally mandated minimum wage laws.

Federal Minimum Wage

Under the Fair Labor Standards Act, an employee has certain rights concerning wages. For example, there is a federal minimum wage requirement which supersedes any state minimum wage laws which would otherwise allow employers to pay employees less than the federal minimum. However, federal minimum wage laws defer to the state's minimum wage law where the state sets a higher minimum wage than the federal government.

Nevertheless, the Department of Labor may issue special certificates that allow the employer to pay less than the minimum wage to certain employees, which may include certain disabled workers and apprentices.

In addition to the minimum wage provisions of the law, overtime pay is mandated as one and one half times the employee's regular rate of pay for all hours worked over 40 in one week.

There are stiff civil and criminal penalties available for employers who do not abide by the law. Employers may be assessed up to $1,000 per violation if they willfully or repeatedly violate the minimum wage or overtime pay provisions of the law. In addition, the Department of Labor may recover back wages for employees who have been underpaid in violation of the law, and those employers found to be in violation may face civil or criminal action against them.

Payroll Taxes

Employers are required to withhold taxes from their employees' salaries, make periodic deposits, and file quarterly payroll tax returns. Employers are responsible for the following withholding taxes:

Federal Income Tax

Federal income tax is money withheld from an employee's earnings based on gross income, number of dependents, marital status, etc.

Federal Unemployment Tax

Federal unemployment taxes are employer-paid taxes.

State Income Tax

Approximately 41 states require the employer to withhold state income tax.

State Unemployment Insurance Tax

State Unemployment Insurance Tax is determined and controlled by the employer and is determined by the company's own unemployment experience.

State Disability Insurance

State Disability Insurance is assessed on employees by some states, and is determined by setting a maximum withholding amount and/or a wage base.

Social Security

Social Security is paid by both the employer and employee. The employer is responsible for collection and payment of the employee's contribution.

Medicare

Medicare is collected on the basis of a percentage of the first $135,000 of income.

CHILD LABOR

The government also regulates the use of child labor. In general, an employee must be at least 16 years of age to work in most non-farm jobs, and at least 18 to work in non-farm occupations which are declared hazardous by the Secretary of Labor. 14 and 15-year old children may work during non-school hours in certain specified positions, provided that they work no more than three hours on a school day or 18 hours in a school week, and no more than eight hours on a non-school day or 40 hours in a non-school week. There are also certain restrictions on the times of day that a child is permitted to work. Violations of the child labor provisions of the law can result in fines of up to $10,000 per child.

For more information concerning the Fair Labor Standards Act and how it applies to your business, contact:

U.S. Department of Labor
Employment Standards Administration
Wage and Hour Division
Washington, D.C. 20210

EQUAL OPPORTUNITY LAW

There are a number of federal laws which prohibit discrimination in the workplace. Different types of employers are subject to different laws, as more fully described below.

Private Employers

Private employers, as well as state and local governments and public or private educational institutions, employment agencies, labor unions, and apprentice programs are subject to the equal opportunity laws listed below. Suspected violations should be reported to:

The U.S. Equal Employment Opportunity Commission (EEOC)
1801 L Street, N.W.
Washington, DC 20507.
Telephone: 1-800-669-EEOC
(TDD): 1-800-800-3302 (for hearing impaired)

Title VII of the Civil Rights Act

Title VII of the Civil Rights Act of 1964, as amended, prohibits discrimination in hiring, promotion, discharge, pay, fringe benefits, and other aspects of employment, on the basis of race, color, religion, sex, or national origin. Most private employers, state and local governments, educational institutions, employment agencies, and labor organizations are subject to Title VII, which covers both current employees and job applicants.

Age Discrimination

The Age Discrimination in Employment Act of 1967 (ADEA), as amended, prohibits discrimination in hiring, promotion, discharge, compensation, terms, conditions, or privileges of employment for persons aged 40 and over. Most private employers, state and local governments, educational institutions, employment agencies and labor organizations are subject to the ADEA, which covers both current employees and job applicants.

The Equal Pay Act

The Equal Pay Act of 1963, as amended, prohibits sex discrimination in payment of wages to women and men who perform substantially equal work in the same establishment. Most private employers are subject to this act, which covers both current employees and job applicants. Although discrimination in pay based on sex is also prohibited by Title VII of the Civil Rights Act, the Equal Pay Act serves to cover employers who may not be subject to Title VII due to the size of the company.

The Americans with Disabilities Act

The Americans with Disabilities Act of 1990 (ADA), as amended, prohibits discrimination in all employment practices, including job application procedures, hiring, firing, compensation, advancement, and other terms and conditions of employment and related activities. Most private employers, state and local governments, educational institutions, employment agencies, and labor organizations are subject to the ADA.

Persons covered under the ADA are defined as qualified individuals with disabilities. In addition, persons who are discriminated against because they know, are associated with, or are related to a disabled individual are also protected. To be "qualified," the person must meet the requirements of the position and be able to perform the essential functions of the position, with or without reasonable accommodation.

A disabled person is defined as a person who has a physical or mental impairment that substantially limits one or more major life activities or a record of such an impairment, or one who is regarded as having such an impairment. Covered infirmities range from paraplegia to AIDS. Minor impairments would not likely be included under the ADA.

In addition to employment-related concerns, businesses which serve the public, such as restaurants, hotels, theaters, and department stores, are also subject to the ADA. Such businesses must make sure their facilities are accessible to the impaired, for example, by widening doorways and installing ramps for wheelchair bound individuals.

Remedies are available to the private individual who encounters violations of the ADA. A lawsuit can be brought by an individual to stop any discriminatory practices. The Attorney General's office is also authorized to bring lawsuits in cases of general public importance. The Attorney General may seek monetary damages and stiff civil penalties, which may not exceed $50,000 for a first violation and $100,000 for any subsequent violation.

Information and ideas concerning modifications under the ADA can be gathered by contacting the various groups that represent the disabled. Information about the requirements affecting public services and accommodations can be obtained from the following office:

Office on the Americans with Disabilities Act
Civil Rights Division
U.S. Department of Justice
P.O. Box 66118
Washington, DC 20035-6118
Telephone: 202-514-0301
(TDD) 202-514-0381/0383 (for hearing impaired)

Federal Contractors or Subcontractors

Employers holding federal contracts or subcontracts are subject to the equal opportunity laws listed below. Suspected violations by employers against applicants to or employees of such companies should be reported to:

The Office of Federal Contract Compliance Programs (OFCCP)
Employment Standards Administration
U.S. Department of Labor

200 Constitution Avenue, N.W.
Washington DC 20210
Telephone: 202-523-9368

Executive Order 11246

Executive Order 11246, as amended, prohibits job discrimination on the basis of race, color, religion, sex, or national origin. This order also requires affirmative action to ensure equality of opportunity in all aspects of employment.

The Rehabilitation Act

Section 503 of the Rehabilitation Act of 1973, as amended, prohibits job discrimination because of handicaps. Section 503 also requires affirmative action by the employer to employ and advance qualified individuals with handicaps who, with reasonable accommodation, can perform the essential functions of a job.

Vietnam Veterans Readjustment Assistance Act

The Vietnam Era Veterans Readjustment Assistance Act of 1974, 38 U.S.C. §4212, prohibits job discrimination and requires affirmative action by the employer to employ and advance qualified Vietnam era veterans and qualified disabled veterans.

EMPLOYEE HEALTH AND SAFETY

In General

All businesses are required to provide a safe and healthy workplace for their employees. Statutes may vary from state to state. Therefore, it is essential that you investigate the particular requirements of your state, as well as the federal regulations promoting health and safety in the workplace, as more fully described below. Small business owners can engage the services of the growing number of workplace safety consultants, who specialize in bringing companies into compliance with the law.

Some safety precautions the small business owner can take include regular in-house safety inspections, a comprehensive safety plan for all employees, and the maintenance of adequate protective clothing and equipment where the nature of business operations requires such precautions. There should also be an adequately stocked first-aid kit readily available, and the telephone numbers for emergency medical assistance should be on display for quick reference if the needs arises.

The Occupational Safety and Health Act

The Occupational Safety and Health Act of 1970 (the Act), provides job safety and health protection for workers by promoting safe and healthful working conditions throughout the nation. The Act is administered by the Occupational Safety and Health Administration (OSHA), a division of the U.S. Department of Labor.

OSHA is responsible for issuing standards relating to the occupational safety and health standards. In addition, OSHA employees conduct routine inspections to determine compliance with the Act. The employer, or an authorized representative of the employer or the employees, is required to accompany the OSHA inspector during such inspections. If the OSHA representative is unable to accompany the representative, the OSHA compliance officer is required to consult with a reasonable number of employees concerning safety and health conditions in the workplace.

Under the Act, employers are required to maintain their facilities free from any recognized hazards that are causing, or are likely to cause, death or serious harm to an employee. On the other hand, employees are also required to comply with all applicable sections of the occupational safety and health standards issued by OSHA.

If a workplace situation exists that appears to be unsafe or unhealthy, a complaint requesting an inspection may be filed with the nearest OSHA office. To encourage compliance, the Act provides that employees who "blow the whistle" by complaining cannot be discharged or discriminated against, and, if they believe that they have suffered discrimination as a result, the employee can file a complaint with the nearest OSHA office within 30 days of the alleged incident.

If an employer is determined to be in violation of the law after an inspection is conducted by an OSHA representative, OSHA may issue a citation against that employer. The citation specifies each and every violation alleged to have been committed by the employer and the date by which the violation must be corrected. The employer is required to display the citation at or near the location of the alleged violation for a period of three days or until the violation is corrected, whichever date is later. The purpose of this provision is to warn the employees about the dangerous condition.

The penalties for failure to adhere to the Act are serious. For example, there are mandatory civil penalties of up to $7,000 per violation against employers for serious violations of the law, and optional penalties of up to $7,000 for nonserious violations. If an employer fails to correct a violation within the allotted time period, additional penalties of up to $7,000 per day can be assessed until the violation is finally corrected.

Willful violations of the Act can result in penalties ranging from a minimum of $5,000 to a maximum of $70,000. Repeated violations can also result in a fine of up to $70,000, and an employer can be assessed a penalty of up to $7,000 for failure to display the citation as required.

In addition to the civil penalties, criminal penalties may be assessed if a willful violation of the Act results in the death of an employee. Upon conviction, such a violation is punishable by a fine of up to $250,000 or by imprisonment of up to six months, or both. If the employer is a corporation, the maximum fine is $500,000. There are additional penalties that may be imposed for subsequent convictions.

OSHA offers free assistance in identifying and correcting workplace safety and health hazards to employers. Employers requesting such assistance are not subject to citation or penalty. OSHA has a 24 hour hotline available for reporting workplace safety and health emergencies (1-800-321-OSHA).

A directory of regional OSHA offices is set forth at Appendix 18.

HANDLING EMPLOYEE THEFT

Employee theft can have a serious detrimental effect on a business. Employee theft can range from stealing petty cash to hiring fictitious personnel and collecting their salaries. Your first defense against employee theft is in the hiring process. You should carefully screen every potential employee, making sure to check the applicant's references. Ideally, a professional background check may save you money in the long run by ruling out a prospective employee who is revealed to be a convicted burglar. The greater the access to company money or other valuables, the more extensive your investigation should be.

An efficient security system should be installed on the premises, as well as a computer security program to detect employee fraud or record tampering. You can also set up a system of checks and balances whereby no one employee has sufficient control over a particular task that they are able to complete the theft. For example, one employee may check invoices for accuracy, and another employee may be responsible for issuing the checks. Nevertheless, you should also be aware of the possibility of collusion among two or more employees.

Employee theft may be discovered in a variety of ways, such as by departmental audits or direct observation. Often, co-workers of the offending employee are aware of the problem, but do not know how to confront the issue. Information on the ethical obligations for the discovery and reporting of suspected employee theft may be included in the employee handbook and made available to all employees, as well as management personnel. The materials may include guidelines that assist the individual in proper and discreet reporting procedures.

If, despite your best efforts, employee theft is suspected, it would be wise to conduct a thorough investigation without making hasty accusations. All relevant documentation should be obtained and carefully reviewed. Conduct confidential interviews with employees who may be able to shed some light on the situation. Take care not to alienate your employees, but encourage them to assist you in resolving the situation. Following the interview, request that the employee interviewed sign a statement outlining the conversation. Give the employee the opportunity to correct the statement, based on his or her recollection of the events.

If your investigation uncovers and identifies employee theft, set up a confidential meeting with the offending employee. A memo outlining the allegations and proposed disciplinary action should be given to the employee, with a space provided for the employee to review the charges and respond in writing. If the employee is terminated, a follow-up letter summarizing the exit interview should be mailed to the employee. It is important to maintain as much documentation as possible concerning the termination of employment in case the company should be sued by the employee at a later date.

THE FAMILY AND MEDICAL LEAVE ACT

The federally mandated Family and Medical Leave Act (FMLA) became effective in August 1993. It provides that employees in companies with 50 employees or more have the right to 12 weeks of unpaid leave in certain situations, such as:

1. Following the birth or adoption of a child, with 30 days advance oral or written notice, unless an emergency arises making advance notice impossible, in which case the employee must notify the employer as soon as possible;

2. To recover from a serious illness; or

3. To care for a seriously ill family member.

In addition, the FMLA provides that the returning employee be placed in the same or an equivalent job, which is defined as one with the same rate of pay, benefits, and conditions of employment, including duties and responsibilities substantially similar to the previous position.

The leave permitted under the FMLA does not have to be taken all at once. For example, it can be used to shorten the work week for the employee who does not want to work full time following the birth of a child. Although companies are not required to pay employees who take leave, they may require or allow employees to apply any paid vacation and sick leave for which they are eligible to the 12 weeks permitted under the FMLA. In addition, state laws which grant rights that are greater than the FMLA supersede the statute.

Many businesses are concerned that employees seeking to take an upaid vacation will simply claim to be seriously ill. However, the FMLA has addressed that possibility by defining "serious illness" as one which requires at least one overnight stay in a hospital or continuing treatment by or under the supervision of a health care worker. Although not required, there are official FMLA medical certification forms available through the U.S. Department of Labor (USDL), Wage and Hour Division. The USDL also hears complaints of violations of the statute. Complaints to the USDL, as well as private lawsuits, must be filed within two years of the alleged violation.

CHAPTER 7:
MAINTAINING BUSINESS RECORDS

IN GENERAL

Keeping accurate, up-to-date records is essential to the smooth operation of any business. Applications, bank statements, bids, by-laws, charters, checks, contracts, internal and external correspondence, employment forms and employee records, expense reports, insurance documents, inventories, invoices, leases, ledgers, licenses, purchase orders, receipts, reports, requisitions, shipping documents, tax returns, and other taxation documents are some of the many records which your company may be required to keep for a specific period of time.

The importance of documenting all aspects of your business operations cannot be stressed. For example, certain records may be referred to for the purpose of assessing the progress of the company. Records may be necessary if litigation arises—for example, regarding employment matters or product liability.

In addition, if taxing authorities question any aspect of your operations, accurate and complete records will assist in satisfying their audit. Thus, it is wise to engage a professional accountant to assist you with accounting and taxation records, particularly if your business operations are complex.

The nature and complexity of the records necessary to effectively manage your business are largely dependent on the type and form of business you operate. This chapter discusses some of the more common business records applicable to the small business.

ACCOUNTING RECORDS

Even though you may need a professional accountant to assist you with your accounting, the small business owner should become familiar with all of the various data and forms that can be used to periodically assess the business. In performing such analysis, the company's income statement is probably the item of primary interest because it reflects the financial condition of the business over a period of time. The income statement contains the company's gross sales, costs, and expenses and gives you information from which you can determine the best method to increase sales and decreases costs.

Other accounting records may include the balance sheet, cash flow analyses, accounts payable and receivable records, and customer account information.

COMPANY FORMATION RECORDS

Depending on the form of business you choose, certain business formation documents will have to be filed and retained. Such documents may include the certificate of incorporation, by-laws, stock certificates, partnership agreements, business registration forms, and tax identification number request forms.

DEPARTMENT OF LABOR RECORDS

The Department of Labor (DOL) oversees and administers many programs and statutory schemes concerning employee-related issues, the most well known of which are the Equal Employment Opportunity Act (EEOA), the Fair Labor Standards Act (FLSA), and the Employee Retirement Income Security Act (ERISA). To comply with many of the DOL regulations, employers are required to maintain on file numerous forms concerning their employees.

EMPLOYEE RECORDS

Unless you have few or no employees, there are many employee-related documents you will need to create and keep on file in addition to those required by the DOL. For example, you will probably have some sort of employee handbook advising employees about such matters as their rights and responsibilities, holidays, benefits, and the merit evaluation process.

In addition, you may have employment contracts, payroll information, hiring forms, and a variety of other employee-related documentation. It is important to keep this information, even after a particular employee departs, in case employment litigation arises. Accurate and complete documentation of your relationship with your employees will assist you in defending any such action.

OSHA RECORDS

As discussed in Chapter 6, employers are responsible to maintain a safe and healthful workplace for their employees. This requirement is overseen by The Occupational Safety and Health Administration (OSHA). Under the Occupational Safety and Health Act, employers are required to report to

OSHA concerning compliance with various prescribed standards of safety and health, entailing additional paperwork for the small business owner.

Although the OSHA records are relatively simple, they are quite important. The required self-reporting documents include a summary and log of occupational injuries and illnesses, which must be filed annually, and a supplemental report describing each incident in detail.

PRODUCT TESTING RECORDS

If you are in the business of manufacturing and distributing products, you must be concerned with keeping records on testing procedures and outcomes. In the event of litigation, these records can be problematic should the testing reports reflect a potential problem related to the subject of the lawsuit.

For example, if a toy truck designed for children aged five and under was tested, and the results showed that, under certain circumstances, small parts of the truck would loosen, those records could be used to support a products liability lawsuit based on a claim that a child choked on one of those small parts. Because the hazard was foreseeable, and the company had prior knowledge of the hazard, it could be found liable for manufacturing and distributing a hazardous product.

TAX RECORDS

As you probably already know from your experience as an individual taxpayer, you cannot avoid Uncle Sam. The Internal Revenue Service, as well as many of the state taxing authorities, require a variety of forms to be filled out and submitted on a timely basis. The consequences of not properly filing the required paperwork with the federal and state taxing authorities can be costly.

BAR CODING

The Uniform Code Council, Inc., a nongovernnment agency, assigns a manufacturer's ID code for the purposes of bar coding. Many stores require bar coding on the packaged products they sell. For additional information concerning a bar code for your small business, contact:

The Uniform Code Council, Inc.
P.O. Box 1244
Dayton, Ohio 45401
Telephone: 513-435-3870.

IRS EMPLOYER TAX IDENTIFICATION NUMBER

An employer who is required to report employment taxes or give tax statements to employees must obtain an employer identification number. For a Federal Tax ID number, please contact the Internal Revenue Service for Form SS4. This Form is available through their web site at http://www.irs.gov. You may call the IRS at 1-800-829-3676 (Publications) and ask for the Small Business Tax Kit #454.

INSURANCE RECORDS

Depending on the type of business you are engaged in, insurance contracts and other documents will compose a large part of your business files. Insurance is defined as a contract whereby, for a stipulated consideration, one party undertakes to compensate the other for loss on a specified subject by specified risks. The party who suffers the loss is known as the insured, and the party who compensates the insured for the loss is known as the insurer, or underwriter. The insurance contract is known as a policy, and the stipulated consideration paid for the policy is called a premium.

For example, a flood insurance policy on your premises will insure your property in case it should be damaged or destroyed in a flood, in which case you will be compensated for the value of the property, up to the amount of insurance you purchased, less any deductible.

Public policy requires that, in order for there to be a valid policy, the insured must have an "insurable interest"—i.e., a right, benefit, or advantage stemming from a property, contract, or relationship, or any liability in respect thereof, that might result in the insured being damaged or suffering a loss if the contemplated risk should occur.

The purpose of this requirement is to deter a person from taking out insurance on property or an individual with which he or she has no connection, for the purpose of gambling on—or actually causing—the destruction or demise of such property or person, in order to collect money. Despite this requirement, it is not unheard of for one with an insurable interest to cause or accelerate the demise of the insured property or person in order to collect the insurance money.

Types of Business Insurance

Depending on the nature of your business, there will be certain risks for which it would be wise to obtain insurance. Some of the types of business-related insurance which may be considered are explained below.

Business Interruption Insurance

Business interruption insurance is designed to cover certain specified expenses of a business while operations have been stopped due to some unforeseen situation. For example, if your business premises are damaged or destroyed by a fire, earthquake, flood, or some other unforeseen reason, certain expenses still need to be paid. These expenses may include employee payroll, taxes, utilities, and other expenses of upkeep during the time your business is being rebuilt.

Catastrophe Insurance

You should insure your premises, and your inventory, against such catastrophes as floods, fires, and earthquakes, or face a total loss should one of these events occur and destroy everything. Each such catastrophe is generally covered under its own policy, e.g., fire insurance, flood insurance, etc.

Crime Insurance

Crime insurance protects the insured from losses incurred as a result of burglary and robbery. Insurance premiums for crime insurance can be reduced if you maintain an alarm system for your business. If your business is located in a high crime area, depending on the state in which you live, you may be eligible for federal crime insurance, administered by the Federal Insurance Administration, which is a division of the Department of Housing and Urban Development (HUD).

Commercial Insurance

Commercial insurance protects and compensates parties to commercial contracts in the case of a breach of contractual obligations on the part of one of the parties.

Employer Insurance

Certain types of insurance are applicable to the employer/employee relationship, as explained below.

Employer Liability Insurance

Employer liability insurance protects the employer against claims made by, or on behalf of, employees who are injured or killed during the course of employment, where such claims are not covered by worker's compensation insurance.

Group Life Term Insurance

Group Life Term Insurance is provided by an employer for a group of employees. The employee does not pay taxes on the premiums paid by the employer. There is no cash value to a group life term insurance policy.

Medical and Hospitalization Insurance

A medical and hospitalization insurance plan is one offered by an employer which covers certain specified illnesses and injuries suffered by employees. The plan can be contributory—wherein the employee contributes to the premium by deductions taken from his or her paycheck—or noncontributory.

Some of the other considerations in devising a medical and hospitalization plan include deductibles, coinsurance payments, benefit limits, and whether the covered persons will include the employee's dependents as well as the employee. The health maintenance organization plan has become popular with both employers and employees, as its costs to the employer are lower than under a major medical policy, and it offers convenience to the employee, although it does take away the individual's right to choose his or her own doctor without restrictions.

Unemployment Insurance

Unemployment insurance is a form of taxation collected from the business which is used to fund unemployment payments and benefits to former employees.

Worker's Compensation Insurance

Worker's compensation insurance compensates employees who are injured in the course of their employment, thereby protecting the employer from having to defend lawsuits brought by such employees. Employers who do not have worker's compensation insurance when required by statute are directly liable to any injured employee.

Fleet Policy Insurance

Fleet policy insurance is a type of blanket policy which covers a number of vehicles owned by the same business.

Key Man Life Insurance

Key man life insurance is purchased by the business on the life of an important or key officer or employee of the business. It is assumed that the business will suffer as a result of the loss of the particular individual thus entitling the business to the proceeds of such insurance upon his or her death.

Liability Insurance

Liability stemming from operation of your business can result in many ways. For example, if an individual is injured as a result of some dangerous or defective condition on your premises, e.g., because of a slip and fall, you may be liable for his or her injuries. In addition, if your employee, in the course of business, causes injury to a third party, you may be liable to the injured person. This could occur, for example, if your employee, while driving a company truck in the course of making a delivery, accidentally strikes a pedestrian. A comprehensive general liability policy can be purchased to cover all risks except those which are specifically enumerated as exclusions.

Malpractice Insurance

Malpractice insurance protects professionals from claims of professional malpractice brought against them. Malpractice insurance is available to many groups of professionals, such as doctors, lawyers, accountants, architects, engineers, and real estate agents.

Partnership Insurance

Partnership insurance is life insurance taken out on the lives of the partners, by the partnership, which is designed to enable the surviving partner to buy out a deceased partner's estate.

Product Liability Insurance

If you are in the business of selling a certain product, you could be found liable to any person who is injured as a result of the use, or foreseeable misuse, of your product.

CHAPTER 8:
OFFICE EQUIPMENT AND TECHNOLOGY

IN GENERAL

Every office requires certain equipment to operate efficiently and cut down on the expense of utilizing outside services. Technological advances have made certain types of equipment, such as photocopiers and computers, available to small business owners, whereas such items were previously cost prohibitive. Many items now have multiple uses, such as the computer/modem set-up, which can send and receive faxes and access the internet, the facsimile machine with copier capabilities, and the answering machine/facsimile/telephone unit. This multi-use capability can reduce the initial cost of essential office equipment.

TELECOMMUNICATIONS

Efficient communication is essential in operating a business. There is a broad range of telephone systems available, each with their own capabilities. The size and nature of your business largely determine the type of telephone system you require to efficiently operate your business. For example, a small, two-person, two-desk office, may not need any more than a two-line telephone system, with one unit for each desk.

A larger business, particularly one which entails sales and marketing, or other heavy telephone usage needs, will require a more complex system. Where inter-office communication is frequent, a system with intercom capabilities can be utilized.

In addition, depending on your location, there are many services available through the local telephone company which may be helpful in operating your business, such as voice mail service, three-way calling, call forwarding, call waiting, caller identification and call return. Check with your local telephone company to find out what services are available in your area.

In any event, since telephone service can become a major company expense, you should devise a telephone use policy to cut down on personal, customer, and long-distance calls. For example, consider installing security devices for efficient monitoring and prevention.

FACSIMILE MACHINE

Another technological advance is the facsimile machine, which has become affordable for the small business owner. The facsimile machine makes it possible to send and receive all types of printed material electronically, using the telephone lines. The faxed material reaches its destination instantaneously, a significant advantage for many businesses.

The facsimile machine is connected to the phone line jack. It may have its own assigned number and line, or it may share a telephone line. If it shares a telephone line, it may be switched on when a facsimile transmission is being sent, or it may automatically receive faxes after a certain number of rings. A device known as a phone/fax switch allows the facsimile machine to determine whether the incoming signal is a caller or a fax. If it is a fax, the machine will respond.

PHOTOCOPIER

No matter what type of business you operate, there is usually a need to make photocopies—e.g. of documents, pictures, checks, invoices, and letters. Copiers can range from small, inexpensive desktop models to larger, more complex machines. Once you have determined the copying requirements of your business, you should find a copier that can meet those needs in the most cost efficient manner. You should take into consideration the purchase price of the copier as well as the cost of processing a copy, including the price of copier cartridges or developing supplies, the paper, and the electricity used by the copier.

If your need for copying is infrequent, it may be cost-effective to spend less for the initial purchase of the copier, even though the per copy processing cost may be relatively high. If your business owns a facsimile machine, it may have copier capabilities, in which case you will not need to purchase a separate copier, as long as the type and quality of the copies made using that machine are sufficient for your needs.

Businesses in which duplicating is a major, frequent undertaking may be better off in the long run buying a more expensive copier with a low per copy processing cost. In the alternative, leasing may be a more cost-effective solution.

COMPUTER SYSTEMS

Every business, small and large, gathers and processes information of some kind. For example, a grocery store owner gathers information on existing inventory to determine what he or she needs to order from suppliers. The cash register has been largely replaced by computerized scanners. A medical office needs to keep appointment, billing, and patient information on file. Before computer technology became available and affordable to the small business owner, this type of record keeping was necessarily done by hand—and preserved on paper—a time-consuming and unreliable method. The computer age has changed the way small companies manage such information. More than 4.5 million small employers (83 percent of all employers) used computer equipment in their operations in 1998.

Purchasing a Computer System

Computer technology advances at a rapid pace. No sooner do you learn how to operate your computer than it is rendered obsolete by an even more efficient unit. Therefore, where cost is a factor, it is important to purchase a computer that will serve all of the foreseeable needs of your company. Before you purchase your computer, you should determine the future needs of your business, including all possible uses of a computer system for your company as it presently exists, and as it may develop and expand.

Engage the assistance of a professional with whom you can discuss your business requirements and who can advise and assist you in purchasing computer hardware and software. If you are not particularly knowledgeable about computers, you may want to purchase a system that is relatively simple to understand and use.

Computer Software

There is software available that covers almost every aspect of business operations, including billing, accounting, payroll, inventory, and scheduling. Before you purchase your computer hardware, review the available software for the different computer models. If you discover software packages that are particularly suited to your company's operations, you should make sure you purchase the proper hardware necessary to run that software. In addition, the experienced computer programmer can create custom-made programs in case certain information processing unique to your business is not available in commercial software.

On-Line Information Services

Many computer data information services provide the user with a variety of information. Such databases are accessed by your computer through your telephone, using a connecting device known as a modem. For example, the Small Business Administration provides an on-line information service to small business owners, known as SBA On-Line. SBA On-Line provides information concerning starting and managing small businesses, including business advice, financing and marketing information, training materials, as well as recent news and laws concerning the small business owner.

Electronic Commerce

According to the Small Business Administration, more small firms are now using electronic commerce. The share of small firms with access to the Internet nearly doubled, from 21.5 percent in 1996 to 41.2 percent in 1998. Small businesses using the Internet have higher revenues, averaging $3.79 million compared with $2.72 million overall.

The Internet is most commonly used by small businesses in insurance agencies, law firms and in other service sectors. E-mail and research—e.g., finding new customers—continue to be the small firms' most popular uses of the Internet.

Online retail marketing is experiencing about 200 percent annual growth, and traffic online has been doubling every 100 days. Nevertheless, internet sales still only account for less than 1 percent of total retail sales. However, by 2002, it is expected that almost one-third of all business-to-business transactions will be via e-commerce.

Cost is small business' major barrier to the adoption of e-commerce. Only 1.4 percent of Internet use among small firms is directed toward e-commerce. In 1997, small firms earned $3.5 billion in e-commerce sales. This is projected to increase to $25 billion by 2002. Doing business on the internet is becoming more attractive to the small business, which can now maintain and design an effective website, reach a wider market, and transact business and accept credit cards on-line for a relatively low cost.

For 78 percent of small business owners, the major reason for having a website is to reach new and potential customers. However, running an e-commerce site can be complicated because there is a lot of competition in the electronic marketplace. Many companies use "hosting services" which maintains their site instead of trying to maintain their web business in-house. There are web hosts who offer complete services, including design of your website, however, the costs are generally prohibitive for a small start-up business.

For very small businesses, one option is to sign up for a Web-based storefront, such as those offered by major servers such as Yahoo. In this way you can test putting your product on-line without expending large sums of money. Generally, you pay a monthly fee for this service. You need to choose and register a "domain name" for your web business. This can be your existing business name if it is available. In order to find out if your desired domain name is free, you can go to http://www.whois.org. It would also be wise to search the U.S. Patent & Trademark Office's database to make sure your intended name does not infringe on any existing trademarks.

In order to run your web business, banks will generally require you to obtain a special Internet Merchant Account, regardless of whether you handle transactions yourself or you have a hosting service. It is important to make sure that you can offer your customers absolute security for their on-line transactions. One way to do so is to get a digital certificate. A digital certificate gives you a secure identity on the internet and enables you to encrypt the messages that pass between you and your customer during transactions. Using a digital certificate to conduct transactions over the internet is very secure provided proper security procedures are followed, e.g., passwords are too easy to guess.

Doing business on the internet allows you to track your customer base in ways not available in traditional marketing. Some companies provide information on which sites receive the most "hits"—the number of times potential customers access the site. You can also have a counter on your website which records the number of hits. Most web servers can also be configured to provide you with information on the last site your customers visited before your site, which may give you some insight into customer needs.

In addition, you can obtain referrals by linking your website with other businesses on the web that sell related products. A link is an imbedded code within your website that will take the customer to the other business's website by clicking on information related to that business, such as their name or product. These type of inter-business advertising agreements can provide an additional source of income if another business is willing to pay you to provide a link to their site on your site.

APPENDIX 1:
WOMEN'S SHARE OF
SELF-EMPLOYMENT—ALL
INDUSTRIES—BY STATE—1997
(THOUSANDS)

STATE	NUMBER	PERCENTAGE OF TOTAL	STATE RANK
United States	3,923	37.3	N/A
Alabama	51	30.5	50
Alaska	13	37.1	29
Arizona	76	46.3	1
Arkansas	43	37.4	28
California	576	36.3	32
Colorado	84	45.7	2
Connecticut	34	31.5	49
Delaware	8	42.1	8
District of Columbia	6	42.9	5
Florida	156	34.1	44
Georgia	83	34.4	40
Hawaii	26	44.1	3
Idaho	27	39.7	15
Illinois	148	38.6	22
Indiana	66	36.1	33
Iowa	57	32.9	45
Kansas	54	40.3	14
Kentucky	56	41.2	12

STATE	NUMBER	PERCENTAGE OF TOTAL	STATE RANK
Louisiana	53	35.6	37
Maine	26	36.6	31
Maryland	74	38.9	18
Massachusetts	90	40.7	13
Michigan	119	41.5	10
Minnesota	104	39.2	17
Mississippi	31	34.1	43
Missouri	102	41.5	11
Montana	26	38.8	21
Nebraska	41	37.6	25
Nevada	21	37.5	26
New Hampshire	23	37.7	24
New Jersey	71	37.0	30
New Mexico	36	41.9	9
New York	187	35.9	34
North Carolina	89	32.1	47
North Dakota	17	32.7	46
Ohio	143	39.6	16
Oklahoma	55	34.2	41
Oregon	74	42.3	7
Pennsylvania	150	34.1	42
Rhode Island	7	28.0	51
South Carolina	39	35.8	36
South Dakota	19	35.8	35
Tennessee	85	31.7	48
Texas	328	38.8	20
Utah	28	35.0	39
Vermont	15	37.5	27
Virginia	75	38.3	23
Washington	115	42.	68

STATE	NUMBER	PERCENTAGE OF TOTAL	STATE RANK
West Virginia	21	38.9	19
Wisconsin	82	35.3	38
Wyoming	13	43.3	4

Source: Small Business Administration; Office of Economic Research.

APPENDIX 2:
SELF-EMPLOYMENT BY RACE AND ETHNIC ORIGIN—1988—1998 (THOUSANDS)

YEAR	TOTAL	WHITE	BLACK	ASIAN	HISPANIC
1988	9,917	9,209	414	294	508
1989	10,008	9,291	411	306	530
1990	10,097	9,377	461	259	523
1991	10,274	9,512	475	287	500
1992	9,960	9,215	452	293	498
1993	10,279	9,487	468	324	543
1994	10,648	9,772	485	391	598
1995	10,482	9,635	512	335	567
1996	10,489	9,577	506	406	644
1997	10,513	9,550	507	456	674
1998	10,303	9,310	533	460	661

Source: Small Business Administration; Office of Advocacy.

APPENDIX 3:
NATIONAL DIRECTORY OF SMALL
BUSINESS ADMINISTRATION OFFICES

STATE	ADDRESS	TELEPHONE NUMBER
ALABAMA	2121 8TH AVENUE NORTH, BIRMINGHAM, AL 35203	205-254-1344
ALASKA	701 C STREET, FEDERAL BUILDING ANNEX, ROOM 1068, ANCHORAGE, AK 99513	907-271-4022
ARIZONA	2005 NORTH CENTRAL AVENUE, PHOENIX, AZ 85004	602-261-3732
ARKANSAS	320 WEST CAPITOL AVENUE, LITTLE ROCK, AR 72201	501-378-5871
CALIFORNIA	2202 MONTEREY STREET, FRESNO, CA 93721	209-487-5189
CALIFORNIA	350 SOUTH FIGUEROA STREET, LOS ANGELES, CA 90071	213-894-2956
CALIFORNIA	880 FRONT STREET, FEDERAL BUILDING, SAN DIEGO, CA 92188	714-293-5430
CALIFORNIA	211 MAIN STREET, SAN FRANCISCO, CA 94105	415-974-0649
COLORADO	721 NINETEENTH STREET, DENVER, CO 80202	303-844-3984
CONNECTICUT	1 HARTFORD SQUARE WEST, HARTFORD, CT 06106	
DELAWARE	844 KING STREET, FEDERAL BUILDING, WILMINGTON, DE 19801	302-573-6294
DISTRICT OF COLUMBIA	1111 18TH STREET N.W., WASHINGTON, DC 20036	202-634-4950

STATE	ADDRESS	TELEPHONE NUMBER
FLORIDA	2222 PONCE DE LEON BLVD., CORAL GABLES, FL 33134	305-350-5521
FLORIDA	400 WEST BAY STREET, JACKSONVILLE, FL 32202	904-791-3784
GEORGIA	1720 PEACHTREE ROAD N.W., ATLANTA, GA 30309	404-881-2441
HAWAII	300 ALA MOANA BLVD., HONOLULU, HI 96850	808-546-8950
IDAHO	1020 MAIN STREET, BOISE, ID 83702	208-334-1696
ILLINOIS	219 SOUTH DEARBORN STREET, CHICAGO, IL 60604	312-353-4528
INDIANA	575 N. PENNSYLVANIA STREET, FEDERAL BUILDING, INDIANAPOLIS, IN 46204	317-269-7272
IOWA	210 WALNUT STREET, FEDERAL BUILDING, DES MOINES, IA 50309	515-284-4422
IOWA	373 COLLINS ROAD NE, CEDAR RAPIDS, IA 52402	319-399-2571
KANSAS	110 EAST WATERMAN STREET, WICHITA, KS 67202	316-269-6616
KENTUCKY	600 FEDERAL PLACE, LOUISVILLE, KY 40201	502-582-5971
LOUISIANA	1661 CANAL STREET, FISK FEDERAL BUILDING, NEW ORLEANS, LA 70112	504-589-6685
MAINE	40 WESTERN AVENUE, AUGUSTA, ME 04330	207-622-8378
MARYLAND	10 NORTH CALVERT STREET, BALTIMORE, MD 21202	301-962-4392
MASSACHUSETTS	150 CAUSEWAY STREET, BOSTON, MA 02114	617-223-4074
MICHIGAN	477 MICHIGAN AVENUE, DETROIT, MI 48226	313-226-6075
MINNESOTA	100 NORTH SIXTH STREET, MINNEAPOLIS, MN 55403	

STATE	ADDRESS	TELEPHONE NUMBER
MISSISSIPPI	100 WEST CAPITOL STREET, FEDERAL BUILDING, JACKSON, MS 39269	601-960-4378
MISSOURI	1103 GRAND AVENUE, KANSAS CITY, MO 64106	
MISSOURI	815 OLIVE STREET, ST. LOUIS, MO 63101	314-425-6600
MONTANA	301 SOUTH PARK STREET, HELENA, MT 59626	406-449-5381
NEBRASKA	EMPIRE STATE BUILDING, 19TH AND FARNAM STREETS, OMAHA, NE 68102	402-221-4691
NEVADA	301 EAST STEWART, LAS VEGAS, NV 89125	702-388-6611
NEW HAMPSHIRE	55 PLEASANT STREET, CONCORD, NH 03301	603-224-4041
NEW JERSEY	60 PARK PLACE, MILITARY PARK BUILDING, NEWARK, NJ 07102	201-645-3580
NEW MEXICO	5000 MARBLE AVENUE NE, ALBUQUERQUE, NM 87110	505-766-3430
NEW YORK	26 FEDERAL PLAZA, NEW YORK, NY 10278	212-264-9487
NEW YORK	100 SOUTH CLINTON STREET, SYRACUSE, NY 13260	315-423-5383
NORTH CAROLINA	230 SOUTH TRYON STREET, CHARLOTTE, NC 28202	704-371-6561
NORTH DAKOTA	653 SECOND AVENUE NORTH, FARGO, ND 58108	701-237-5771
OHIO	1240 EAST NINTH STREET, CLEVELAND, OH 44199	216-522-4180
OHIO	85 MARCONI BOULEVARD, FEDERAL BUILDING, COLUMBUS, OH 43215	614-469-6860
OKLAHOMA	200 NORTHWEST FIFTH STREET, FEDERAL BUILDING, OKLAHOMA CITY, OK 73102	405-231-4301
OREGON	1220 SOUTHWEST THIRD AVENUE, FEDERAL BUILDING, PORTLAND, OR 97204	503-221-2682

STATE	ADDRESS	TELEPHONE NUMBER
PENNSYLVANIA	ONE BALA CYNWYD PLAZA, 231 ST. ASAPHS ROAD, BALACYNWYD, PA 19004	215-596-5889
PENNSYLVANIA	960 PENN AVENUE, PITTSBURGH, PA 15222	412-644-2780
RHODE ISLAND	380 WESTMINSTER MALL, PROVIDENCE, RI 02903	401-528-4580
SOUTH CAROLINA	1835 ASSEMBLY STREET, COLUMBIA, SC 29202	803-765-5373
SOUTH DAKOTA	101 SOUTH MAIN AVENUE, SIOUX FALLS, SD 57102	605-336-2980
TENNESSEE	404 JAMES ROBERTSON PARKWAY, NASHVILLE, TN 37219	615-251-5881
TEXAS	1100 COMMERCE STREET, DALLAS, TX 75242	214-767-0605
TEXAS	10737 GATEWAY WEST, EL PASO, TX 79935	915-541-7678
TEXAS	222 EAST VAN BUREN, HARLINGEN, TX 78550	512-423-8934
TEXAS	2525 MURWORTH, HOUSTON, TX 77054	713-660-4401
TEXAS	1611 10TH STREET, LUBBOCK, TX 79401	806-743-7462
TEXAS	727 EAST DURANGO, FEDERAL BUILDING, SAN ANTONIO, TX 78206	512-229-6250
UTAH	125 SOUTH STATE STREET, SALT LAKE CITY, UT 84138	801-524-5800
VERMONT	87 STATE STREET, MONTPELIER, VT 05602	802-229-0538
VIRGINIA	400 NORTH EIGHTH STREET, FEDERAL BUILDING, RICHMOND, VA 23240	804-771-2741
WASHINGTON	915 SECOND AVENUE, FEDERAL BUILDING, SEATTLE, WA 98174	206-442-5534
WASHINGTON	651 U.S. COURTHOUSE, 920 RIVERSIDE AVENUE, SPOKANE, WA 99210	509-456-3786

STATE	ADDRESS	TELEPHONE NUMBER
WEST VIRGINIA	168 WEST MAIN STREET, CLARKSBURG, WV 26302	304-623-5631
WISCONSIN	212 EAST WASHINGTON AVENUE, MADISON, WI 53703	608-264-5261
WYOMING	100 EAST B STREET, FEDERAL BUILDING, CASPER, WY 82602	307-261-5761
PUERTO RICO/VIRGIN ISLANDS	CARLOS CHARDON AVENUE, FEDERAL BUILDING, HATO REY, PR 00918	809-753-4520

APPENDIX 4:
BUSINESS CERTIFICATE

I hereby certify that I am conducting or transacting business under the name or designation of [Name of Company], at [address of Company].

My full name is [Name of Owner], and I reside at [Owner's Address].

IN WITNESS WHEREOF, I have made and signed this certificate on [date].

Signature Line for Owner

STATE OF _____

COUNTY OF _____

On [date], before me personally came [owner's name], to me known to be the person described in and who executed the foregoing instrument and duly acknowledged to me that (s)he executed the same.

Signature Line for Notary

APPENDIX 5:
PARTNERSHIP AGREEMENT

This Agreement dated July 1, 2001, is by and between John Smith, of 123 Main Street, City, State, 00000, Mary Jones of 321 Central Avenue, City, State 00000, and Jane Doe of 1010 First Avenue, City, State 00000.

The parties agree to carry on business as a partnership, as follows:

ARTICLE ONE: PURPOSE

1. The purpose of the partnership is (state purpose).

ARTICLE TWO: NAME

2. The name of the partnership is Smith, Jones & Doe.

ARTICLE THREE: TERM

3. The partnership will begin as of the date first written above, and will continue indefinitely until terminated.

4. The partnership may be terminated by a a majority vote of the partners.

ARTICLE FOUR: CONTRIBUTIONS

5. Each partner will contribute the following property, services or cash to the partnership, as follows:

   a) John Smith—(describe contribution).

   b) Mary Jones—(describe contribution).

   c) Jane Doe—(describe contribution).

ARTICLE FIVE: BANK ACCOUNT

6. The partnership will open and maintain a bank account in the National Bank, located at 456 Main Street, City, State 00000.

7. Check-signing privileges are as follows:

a) Checks under $100.00 may be authorized and signed by any individual partner;

b) Checks from $100.00 to $500.00 require the authorization and signature of two partners;

c) Checks over $500.00 require the authorization and signature of all partners.

ARTICLE SIX: OWNERSHIP

8. The profits and losses of the partnership will be shared by both partners as follows:

a) John Smith—33-1/3%

b) Mary Jones—33-1/3%

c) Jane Doe—33-1/3%

ARTICLE SEVEN: MANAGEMENT

9. All partners will have an equal right to manage the partnership.

10. Partnership decisions will be made by majority vote.

ARTICLE EIGHT: ACCOUNTING

11. The partnership will maintain accounting records at the following location (specify location).

12. Each partner will have the right to inspect such accounting records at any time.

ARTICLE NINE: WITHDRAWAL

13. Upon the withdrawal from the partnership of any partner, or the death of any partner, the partnership will continue and will be managed by the surviving partners.

ARTICLE TEN: PARTNERSHIP INTEREST

14. A partner's interest in the partnership may not be transferred, in whole or in part, to any other party.

15. Upon the withdrawal from the partnership of any partner, or upon the death of any partner, that partner's interest in the partnership shall be sold to the remaining partners, in equal shares, and the remaining partners

will be required to buy that interest, the value of which will be the departing partner's proportionate share of the total value of the partnership.

ARTICLE ELEVEN: WINDING UP

16. Upon termination of the partnership, the partners agree to distribute partnership assets in the following order:

a) Debts of the partnership shall be paid;

b) Income accounts shall be distributed to each partner in his or her proportionate share.

c) Capital accounts shall be distributed to each partner in his or her proportionate share.

d) Any remaining partnership assets shall be distributed to each partner in his or her proportionate share.

ARTICLE TWELVE: MISCELLANEOUS PROVISIONS

17. This agreement contains the entire understanding of the partners.

18. Any modification of this agreement must be in writing and signed by all of the partners.

19. This Agreement is being made in [Name of State] and shall be construed and enforced according to the laws of that state.

20. Additional Terms (specify):

IN WITNESS WHEREOF, the parties have duly executed this Agreement as of the date first written above.

Signature Line for John Smith, Partner

Signature Line for Mary Jones, Partner

Signature Line for Jane Doe, Partner

APPENDIX 6:
CERTIFICATE OF INCORPORATION OF [CORPORATE NAME]

It is hereby certified that:

1. The name of the proposed corporation is: [insert name].

2. The office of the corporation is to be located in: [insert address of corporation].

3. This corporation is for the following purposes: [insert specific purposes or use all-inclusive clause as follows] To engage in any lawful activity for which corporations may be organized under the laws of the State of [Name of State].

4. The total number of shares which the corporation shall have the authority to issue is: [insert number of authorized shares].

5. The par value of each share of stock is: [insert value of stock].

In witness whereof, this certificate has been subscribed on [insert date] by the undersigned who affirm that the statements made herein are true under the penalties of perjury.

Signature Line for Incorporator

Address Line for Incorporator

APPENDIX 7:
SECTION 1244 STOCK DESIGNATION CLAUSE

The Board of Directors have determined that in order to attract investment in the corporation, the corporation shall be organized and managed so that it is a Small Business Corporation" as defined in §1244(c)(1) of the Internal Revenue Code, and so that the shares issued by the corporation are §1244 Stock as defined in §1244(c)(1) of the Internal Revenue Code. Compliance with this section will enable shareholders to treat the loss on the sale or exchange of their shares as an ordinary loss on their personal income tax returns.

It is resolved, that the proper officers of the corporation are authorized to sell and issue common shares in the aggregate amount of money and other property (as a contribution to capital and as paid in surplus), which together with the aggregate amount of common shares outstanding at the time of issuance, does not exceed $1,000,000, and

It is resolved that the sale and issuance of shares shall be conducted in compliance with §1244 of the Internal Revenue Code, so that the corporation and its shareholders may obtain the benefits of §1244 of the Internal Revenue Code, and further

It is resolved that the proper officers of the corporation are directed to maintain such accounting records as are necessary so that any shareholder that experiences a loss on the transfer of common shares of the corporation may determine whether they qualify for ordinary loss deduction treatment on their personal income tax returns.

APPENDIX 8:
COMMERCIAL LEASE AGREEMENT

This Lease is made on July 1, 2001, by and between ABC Properties (Landlord), with offices located at 500 Main Street, City, State 00000, and John Smith d/b/a Smith's Grocery Store (Tenant), of 123 Main Street, City, State 00000. For valuable consideration, the parties agree as follows:

ARTICLE ONE: DESCRIPTION OF PROPERTY

1. The Landlord agrees to rent to the Tenant the following commercial property:

   a) Property Address:

   b) Description of Property:

   c) Square Feet:

ARTICLE TWO: LEASE TERM

2. The term of this lease will commence on July 1, 2001, until July 1, 2002. Tenant will take immediate possession of the property.

ARTICLE THREE: RENT

3. The monthly rent for the property is [Insert $ Amount] per square foot for a total monthly rent of [Insert $ Amount], the first payment of which is due upon execution of this lease agreement.

4. Rent is payable on the first of each month.

5. There is a grace period of 15 days after which time a late fee in the amount of [Insert $ Amount] will be assessed.

6. If Tenant fails to pay rent on time, Landlord has the right to terminate this lease agreement.

ARTICLE FOUR: CONDITION OF PROPERTY

7. Tenant has inspected the premises and has found the property to be in satisfactory condition. Tenant agrees to maintain the property in such condition, and to return the property to Landlord, upon expiration of this Lease, in the same condition as when it was first leased by Tenant, and to be responsible for any damages sustained to the property by Tenant during the term of the lease, except for normal wear and tear.

8. Landlord agrees to be responsible for the repair and upkeep of the property exterior and Tenant agrees to be responsible for the repair and upkeep of the property interior.

ARTICLE FIVE: DEPOSITS

9. Upon execution of this lease, Tenant will deposit with Landlord the sum of [Insert $ Amount], which represents a security deposit which will be returned to Tenant within 15 days after termination of the Lease, minus any amounts deducted to cover the repair of any damages sustained to the premises by Tenant, according to Article Four above.

10. Upon execution of this lease, Tenant will deposit with Landlord the sum of [Insert $ Amount], which represents one additional month's rent which will be returned to Tenant within 15 days after termination of the Lease, minus any amounts deducted for rent still outstanding upon termination.

ARTICLE SIX: SERVICES/UTILITIES

11. The Landlord agrees to supply the following services and utilities to Tenant during the term of this lease: (specify)

ARTICLE SEVEN: SUBLEASING

12. Tenant shall not sublet the property without Landlord's written consent, which shall not be unreasonably withheld.

ARTICLE EIGHT: MISCELLANEOUS PROVISIONS

13. This agreement contains the entire understanding of the partners.

14. Any modification of this agreement must be in writing and signed by all of the partners.

15. This Sublease binds and benefits both parties and any successors.

16. Additional Provisions (specify):

Signature Line for Landlord ABC Properties

Signature Line for Tenant John Smith d/b/a Smith's Grocery Store

APPENDIX 9:
SUBLEASE AGREEMENT

This Lease is made on July 1, 2001, by and between John Smith (Tenant), of 123 Main Street, City, State 00000, and Mary Jones (Sub-tenant), of 456 Central Avenue, City, State 00000.

For valuable consideration, the parties agree as follows:

ARTICLE ONE: DESCRIPTION OF PROPERTY

1. The Tenant agrees to sublease to the Sub-tenant the following property:

   a) Property Address:

   b) Description of Property:

ARTICLE TWO: CURRENT TERMS AND CONDITIONS

2. The above-described property is currently leased to Tenant under the terms of the following described lease, a copy of which is attached hereto: (describe terms and conditions of current lease)

ARTICLE THREE: SUBLEASE TERM

3. The term of this sublease will commence on July 1, 2001, until July 1, 2002. Sub-tenant will take immediate possession of the property.

ARTICLE FOUR: RENT

4. The monthly subrental payment for the property is [Insert $ Amount] per month, the first payment of which is due upon execution of this lease agreement.

5. Rent is payable on the first of each month.

ARTICLE FIVE: MISCELLANEOUS PROVISIONS

6. Tenant represents that the underlying lease agreement is in effect and permission to sublet this property is authorized. A copy of such permission from Landlord is attached hereto.

7. Tenant agrees to indemnify and hold Sub-tenant harmless from any claim which may result from Tenant's failure to perform under Tenant this lease prior to execution of this Sublease.

8. Sub-tenant agrees to indemnify and hold Tenant harmless from any claim which may result from Sub-tenant's failure to perform under the this lease subsequent to execution of this Sublease.

9. Sub-tenant agrees to perform all obligations and duties of Tenant under the original lease, and sub-tenant shall receive all benefits of Tenant under the original lease.

10. Tenant agrees to remain liable to Landlord for all obligations under the terms and conditions of the original lease.

11. This agreement contains the entire understanding of the partners.

12. Any modification of this agreement must be in writing and signed by all of the partners.

13. This Sublease binds and benefits both parties and any successors.

14. Additional Provisions (specify):

Signature Line for Tenant John Smith

Signature Line for Sub-tenant Mary Jones

APPENDIX 10:
TOP 55 COMMERCIAL BANKS PROVIDING LOANS TO SMALL BUSINESSES

RANK	BANK NAME	HEADQUARTERS
1.	BB&T CORPORATION	WINSTON-SALEM NC
2.	U.S. BANCORP	MINNEAPOLIS MN
3.	UNION PLANTERS CORPORATION	MEMPHIS TN
4.	REGIONS FINANCIAL CORPORATION	BIRMINGHAM AL
5.	WELLS FARGO & COMPANY	SAN FRANCISCO CA
6.	ZIONS BANCORPORATION	SALT LAKE CITY UT
7.	SYNOVUS FINANCIAL CORP.	COLUMBUS GA
8.	HUNTINGTON BANCSHARES INCORP.	COLUMBUS OH
9.	FIRST AMERICAN CORPORATION	NASHVILLE TN
10.	SOUTHTRUST CORPORATION	BIRMINGHAM AL
11.	COLONIAL BANCGROUP INC.	MONTGOMERY AL
12.	NATIONAL CITY CORPORATION	CLEVELAND OH
13.	FIRSTAR CORPORATION	MILWAUKEE WI
14.	MARSHALL & ILSLEY CORPORATION	MILWAUKEE WI
15.	KEYCORP	CLEVELAND OH
16.	BANK ONE CORPORATION	CHICAGO IL
17.	COMPASS BANCSHARES INC.	BIRMINGHAM AL
18.	AMSOUTH BANCORPORATION	BIRMINGHAM AL
19.	SUNTRUST BANKS INC.	ATLANTA GA
20.	M&T BANK CORPORATION	BUFFALO NY
21.	BANK OF AMERICA CORPORATION	CHARLOTTE NC
22.	MERCANTILE BANCORPORATION	SAINT LOUIS MO

RANK	BANK NAME	HEADQUARTERS
23.	WACHOVIA CORPORATION	WINSTON-SALEM NC
24.	FIRST UNION CORPORATION	CHARLOTTE NC
25.	HIBERNIA CORPORATION	NEW ORLEANS LA
26.	COMERICA INCORPORATED	DETROIT MI
27.	FIRST SECURITY CORPORATION	SALT LAKE CITY UT
28.	FIRST TENNESSEE NATIONAL	MEMPHIS TN
29.	OLD KENT FINANCIAL CORPORATION	GRAND RAPIDS MI
30.	ASSOCIATED BANC-CORP	GREEN BAY WI
31.	CITIGROUP INC.	NEW YORK NY
32.	CHASE MANHATTAN CORPORATION	NEW YORK NY
33.	FIFTH THIRD BANCORP	CINCINNATI OH
34.	HSBC BK USA	BUFFALO NY
35.	COMMERCE BANCSHARES INC.	KANSAS CITY MO
36.	FLEET FINANCIAL GROUP INC.	BOSTON MA
37.	PNC BANK CORP.	PITTSBURGH PA
38.	NORTH FORK BANCORPORATION	MELVILLE NY
39.	ALLFIRST BANK	BALTIMORE MD
40.	MICHIGAN NB	FARMINGTON HILLS MI
41.	SUMMIT BANCORP.	PRINCETON NJ
42.	PACIFIC CENTURY FINANCIAL CO.	HONOLULU HI
43.	MELLON BANK CORPORATION	PITTSBURGH PA
44.	UNION BANK OF CALIFORNIA	SAN FRANCISCO CA
45.	LASALLE BANK	CHICAGO IL
46.	BANCWEST CORPORATION	HONOLULU HI
47.	BANK OF NEW YORK COMPANY	NEW YORK NY
48.	TCF FINANCIAL CORPORATION	WAYZATA MN
49.	BANK OF BOSTON CORPORATION	BOSTON MA
50.	HARRIS T&SB	CHICAGO IL
51.	NORTHERN TRUST CORPORATION	CHICAGO IL
52.	REPUBLIC NEW YORK CORPORATION	NEW YORK NY
53.	STATE STREET CORPORATION	BOSTON MA

RANK	BANK NAME	HEADQUARTERS
54.	J.P. MORGAN & company INCORPORATED	NEW YORK NY
55.	BANKERS TRUST COMPANY	NEW YORK NY

Source: U.S. Small Business Administration, Office of Advocacy, Office of Economic Research.

APPENDIX 11:
BUSINESS PLAN

COVER PAGE

The cover page should contain the basic information about your company, including the name, address and telephone number of the company, and the contact person. You can also include a space to input the name of the person to whom you are giving a copy of your business plan and the date sent.

PART 1: INVESTOR FUNDS

This section should discuss the type of investment being offered, e.g., stock, etc., and the total percentage of ownership that is being offered. Explain why the company is seeking additional financing, e.g., to increase manufacturing capabilities, to expand its market, etc., and show how those funds will be used. Include sections which explain the risks involved, and the potential return on the investment.

PART 2: ABOUT THE COMPANY

This section summarizes the background and goals of the company. Describe the historical background of your company, including the date of organization, legal structure, and, if incorporated, the date and state of incorporation. Discuss the product or service, and the company's track record, if any, in the particular business. Explain why this company is expected to succeed.

PART 3: ABOUT THE PRODUCT (OR SERVICE)

This section should include a detailed description of the product or service, including the costs involved, such as the costs of research and development, manufacturing, and distribution. Also discuss your pricing plans, the sales projections, and potential profits. Compare and differentiate your product or service from those already available. If your product or service is unique, explain why. Include information concerning the legal status of your product, such as patent and trademark protection.

PART 4: THE MARKET

This section should discuss all aspects of the market for the product or service. Detail the overall size and nature of the market, as well as your targeted market segment. Provide hard statistical data that indicates a growing need for your particular product or service. Discuss why the product or service your company offers will be competitive in the market, and differentiate your product or service from those of other companies in the same type of business. Describe your marketing plan, including the established methods of advertising, distribution, and sales. If your product or service is unique, explain what needs it will fulfill and why it will succeed. In addition, discuss future growth and the possible crossover into new markets.

PART 5: COMPANY MANAGEMENT AND PERSONNEL

This section should list your company's management personnel and supporting staff. Discuss each manager's background, accomplishments and experience, and how they will contribute to the success of the company, and state the level of compensation. If any manager has had prior success in the particular business, point that out as well. This section should also include an organizational chart of the various departments of your company, the key support personnel in each department, and their job descriptions.

PART 6: OWNERSHIP AND CONTROL

This section should discuss ownership and control of the company. Discuss the principal's experience in the particular field and qualifications. If applicable, include a list of the stockholders of your company and how they acquired their equity. If there is a board of directors, list the members and their relevant backgrounds.

PART 8: FINANCIAL ANALYSIS

This section should summarize the company's financial condition, including capital contributions and outstanding debt. Detail the prior use of funds, such as research and development, advertising, manufacturing and distribution costs, and working capital. Include documentation of past performance of the company.

PART 9: RISK ANALYSIS

This section should include an analysis of the risks, including the methods undertaken to reduce such risks. Outline and discuss various financial scenarios, including the worst-case and best-case scenarios.

PART 10: STRATEGIES, OBJECTIVES, AND GOALS

This section should discuss your operating plan, including your specific strategies, objectives, and short-term and long-term goals. Outline the objectives you wish to accomplish at various intervals—e.g., quarterly—and your ultimate goal. Include your financial projections for the next 5 years.

APPENDICES

The appendices may include copies of the newspaper clippings, resumes, statistical data, financial tables, etc., which support the various parts of the plan.

APPENDIX 12:
SBA FORM 770—FINANCIAL STATEMENT OF DEBTOR

U.S. SMALL BUSINESS ADMINISTRATION
FINANCIAL STATEMENT OF DEBTOR
(INSERT THE WORD "NONE" WHERE APPLICABLE TO ANY OF THE FOLLOWING ITEMS)

1. NAME	2. DATE OF BIRTH (Month, Day and Year)	
3. ADDRESS (Include ZIP Code)	4. PHONE NO.	5. SOCIAL SEC. NO.
6. OCCUPATION SBA LOAN NUMBER	7. HOW LONG IN PRESENT	
8. EMPLOYER'S NAME ADDRESS (Include ZIP Code)	PHONE NUMBER	

9. MONTHLY INCOME:
Salary or wages $ _____
Commissions $ _____
Other (state source) $ _____
Total $ _____

10. OTHER EMPLOYERS WITHIN LAST 3 YEARS

Name	Address	Dates of Employment

11. NAME OF SPOUSE	SOCIAL SEC. NO.	12. DATE OF BIRTH (Month, Day and Year)
13. OCCUPATION		14. HOW LONG IN PRESENT
15. SPOUSE'S EMPLOYER (Name)	ADDRESS (Include ZIP Code)	PHONE NUMBER

16. MONTHLY INCOME OF SPOUSE:
Salary or wages $ _____
Commissions $ _____
Other (state source) $ _____
Total $ _____

17. OTHER EMPLOYERS WITHIN LAST 3 YEARS (Of Spouse)

Name	Address	Dates of Employment

18. OTHER DEPENDENTS: _____ NUMBER

Name	Relationship	Age

19. TOTAL MONTHLY INCOME OF DEPENDENTS (Except Spouse)
$ _____

20. FOR WHAT PERIOD DID YOU LAST FILE A FEDERAL INCOME TAX RETURN?

21. WHERE WAS TAX RETURN FILED?

22. AMOUNT OF GROSS INCOME REPORTED
$ _____

23. FIXED MONTHLY EXPENSES: (TO NEAREST DOLLAR)

Rent or House Payment	$ _____
Utilities	$ _____
Food	$ _____
Interest	$ _____
Insurance	$ _____
Debt repayments:	
Household furnishings	$ _____
Personal Loans	$ _____
Automobile	$ _____
Doctors and Dentist	$ _____
Other (Specify)	$ _____
TOTAL FIXED MONTHLY EXPENSES	$ _____

(SHOW AMOUNTS TO NEAREST)

24. ASSETS: (Fair Market Value)		LIABILITIES	
Cash			
Checking accounts: (Show location)	$	Bills owed (grocery, doctor, lawyer, etc.)	$
Savings Accounts: (Show location)		Installment debt (car, furniture, clothing, etc.)	
		Taxes owed:	
Cash surrender value of life insurance		Income	
Motor Vehicles:		Other: (Itemize)	
Make Year License No.			
		Loans payable (to banks, finance companies, etc.)	
Debts owed to you: (Name of debtor)		Judgments you owe (Held by whom?)	
Stocks, bonds and other securities: (Itemize)		Small Business Administration	
		Loans on Life Insurance	
Household furniture and goods		Mortgages on Real Estate	
Items Used in Trade or Business		Margin Payable on Securities	
Other Personal Property: (Itemize)		Other debts: (Itemize)	
Real Estate: (Itemize)			
Other Assets: (Itemize)		Total Liabilities	$
TOTAL ASSETS:	$	CONTINGENT LIABILITIES	$

SBA FORM 770 (1-87) SOP 50 51 USE 3-85 EDITION UNTIL EXHAUSTED   This form was electronically produced by Elite Federal Forms, Inc.   PAGE 1

---

25. LOANS PAYABLE: Owed To	Date of Loan	Original Amount	Present Balance	Terms of Repayments	How Secured
		$	$	$	
		$	$	$	
		$	$	$	

26. REAL ESTATE OWNED: (Free & Clear) Address	How Owned (Jointly, individually, etc.)	Present Market Value $

27. REAL ESTATE BEING PURCHASED ON CONTRACT OR MORTGAGE Address	Date acquired	Balance Owed $
	Name of Seller or Mortgagor	
	Purchase Price $	Date Next Cash Payment Due
	Present Market Value $	Amount of Next Cash Payment $

28. LIFE INSURANCE POLICIES: Company	Face Amount	Cash Surrender Value	Outstanding Loans
	$	$	$
	$	$	$
	$	$	$

29. LIST ALL REAL AND PERSONAL PROPERTY OWNED BY SPOUSE AND DEPENDENTS VALUED IN EXCESS OF $200:

30. LIST ALL TRANSFERS OF PROPERTY, INCLUDING CASH (BY LOAN, GIFT, SALE, ETC.), THAT YOU HAVE MADE WITHIN THE LAST THREE YEARS. (LIST ONLY TRANSFERS OF $300 OR OVER.) Property Transferred	To Whom	Date	Amount
			$
			$
			$

31. ARE YOU A CO-MAKER, GUARANTOR, OR A PARTY IN ANY LAW SUIT OR CLAIM NOW PENDING? ☐ YES ☐ NO IF YES, GIVE DETAILS

32. ARE YOU A TRUSTEE, EXECUTOR, OR ADMINISTRATOR? ☐ YES ☐ NO IF YES, GIVE DETAILS

33. ARE YOU A BENEFICIARY UNDER A PENDING, OR POSSIBLE, INHERITANCE OR TRUST, PENDING OR ESTABLISHED? NO ☐ YES ☐ IF YES, GIVE DETAILS

34. WHEN DO YOU FEEL THAT YOU CAN START MAKING PAYMENTS ON YOUR SBA DEBT?

35. HOW MUCH DO YOU FEEL THAT YOU CAN PAY SBA ON A MONTHLY OR PERIODIC BASIS?

With knowledge of the penalties for false statements provided by 18 United States Code 1001 ($10,000 fine and/or five years imprisonment) and with knowledge that this financial statement is submitted by me to affect action by the Government, I certify that all the above statement is true and that it is a complete statement of all my income and assets, real and personal, whether held in my name or by another.

Under the provisions of the Privacy Act, loan applicants are not required to give their social security number. The Small Business Administration, however, uses the social security number to distinguish between people with a similar or the same name. Failure to provide this number may not affect any right, benefit or privilege to which an individual is entitled by law but having the number makes it easier for SBA to more accurately identify to whom adverse credit information applies and to keep accurate loan records.

Any Person concerned with the collection of this information, its voluntariness, disclosure or routine under the Privacy Act may contact the Freedom of Information/Privacy Acts Division, Small Business Administration, 409 3rd St., S.W., Washington, D.C. 20416

SIGNATURE	DATE

NOTE: USE ADDITIONAL SHEETS WHERE SPACE ON THIS FORM IS INSUFFICIENT.

PAGE 2

SBA FORM 770 (1-87) SOP 50 51 USE 3-85 EDITION UNTIL EXHAUSTED

APPENDIX 13:
SBA FORM 4—APPLICATION FOR BUSINESS LOAN

	U.S. Small Business Administration **APPLICATION FOR BUSINESS LOAN**	OMB Approval No: 3245-0016 Expiration Date: 9/30/01

Individual	Full Address	

Name of Applicant Business		Tax I.D. No. or SSN
Full Street Address of Business		Tel. No. (inc. A/C)

City	County	State	Zip	Number of Employees (Including subsidiaries and affiliates)
Type of Business		Date Business Established		At Time of Application ____
Bank of Business Account and Address				If Loan is Approved ____
				Subsidiaries or Affiliates (Separate for above) ____

Use of Proceeds: (Enter Gross Dollar Amounts Rounded to the Nearest Hundreds)	Loan Requested			Loan Request
Land Acquisition		Payoff SBA Loan		
New Construction/ Expansion Repair		Payoff Bank Loan (Non SBA Associated		
Acquisition and/or Repair of Machinery and Equipment		Other Debt Payment (Non SBA Associated)		
Inventory Purchase		All Other		
Working Capital (including Accounts Payable)		Total Loan Requested		
Acquisition of Existing Business		Term of Loan - (Requested Mat.)		____ Yrs.

PREVIOUS SBA OR OTHER FEDERAL GOVERNMENT DEBT: If you or any principals or affiliates have 1) ever requested Government Financing or 2) are delinquent on the repayment of any Federal Debt complete the following:

Name of Agency	Original Amount of Loan	Date of Request	Approved or Declined	Balance	Current or Past Due
	$			$	
	$			$	

ASSISTANCE List the name(s) and occupation of anyone who assisted in the preparation of this form, other than applicant.

Name and Occupation	Address	Total Fees Paid	Fees Due
Name and Occupation	Address	Total Fees Paid	Fees Due

Note: The estimated burden completing this form is 12.0 hours per response. You will not be required to respond to any collection of information unless it displays a currently valid OMB approval number. Comments on the burden should be sent to U.S. Small Business Administration, Chief, AIB, 409 3rd St., S.W., Washington, D.C. 20416 and Desk Office for Small Business Administration, Office of Management and Budget, New Executive Office Building, room 10202 Washington, D.C. 20503. OMB Approval (3245-0016).PLEASE DO NOT SENDFORMS TO OMB. SUBMIT COMPLETED APPLICATION TO LENDER OF CHOICE

SBA Form 4 (3-00) Previous Edition Obsolete

This form was electronically produced by Elite Federal Forms, Inc.

Page 1

ALL EXHIBITS MUST BE SIGNED AND DATED BY PERSON SIGNING THIS FORM

BUSINESS INDEBTEDNESS: Furnish the following information on all installment debts, contracts, notes, and mortgages payable. Indicate by an asterisk (*) items to be paid by loan proceeds and reason for paying them (present balance should agree with the latest balance sheet submitted).

To Whom Payable	Original Amount	Original Date	Present Balance	Rate of Interest	Maturity Date	Monthly Payment	Security	Current or Past Due
Acct. #	$		$			$		
Acct. #	$		$			$		
Acct. #	$		$			$		
Acct. #	$		$			$		
Acct. #	$		$			$		

MANAGEMENT (Proprietor, partners, officers, directors, all holders of outstanding stock – 100% of ownership must be shown). Use separate sheet if necessary.

Name and Social Security Number and Position Title	Complete Address	%Owned	*Military Service From To	*Sex

Race*: American Indian/Alaska Native ☐   Black/African-Amer. ☐   Asian ☐   Native Hawaiian/Pacific Islander ☐   White ☐   Ethnicity* Hispanic ☐   Not Hispanic ☐

Race*: American Indian/Alaska Native ☐   Black/African-Amer. ☐   Asian ☐   Native Hawaiian/Pacific Islander ☐   White ☐   Ethnicity* Hispanic ☐   Not Hispanic ☐

Race*: American Indian/Alaska Native ☐   Black/African-Amer. ☐   Asian ☐   Native Hawaiian/Pacific Islander ☐   White ☐   Ethnicity* Hispanic ☐   Not Hispanic ☐

Race*: American Indian/Alaska Native ☐   Black/African-Amer. ☐   Asian ☐   Native Hawaiian/Pacific Islander ☐   White ☐   Ethnicity* Hispanic ☐   Not Hispanic ☐

*This data is collected for statistical purpose only. It has no bearing on the credit decision to approve or decline this application.

THE FOLLOWING EXHIBITS MUST BE COMPLETED WHERE APPLICABLE. ALL QUESTIONS ANSWERED ARE MADE A PART OF THE APPLICATION.

For Guarantee Loans please provide an original and one copy (Photocopy is Acceptable) of the Application Form, and all Exhibits to the participating lender. For Direct Loans submit one original copy of the application and Exhibits to SBA.

1. Submit SBA Form 912 (Statement of Personal History) for each type of individual that the Form 912 requires.

2. If your collateral consists of (A) Land and Building, (B) Machinery and Equipment, (C) Furniture and Fixtures, (D) Accounts Receivable, (E) Inventory, (F) Other, please provide an itemized list (labeled Exhibit A) that contains serial and identification numbers for all articles that had an Original value of greater than $500. Include a legal description of Real Estate Offered as collateral.

3. Furnish a signed current personal balance sheet (SBA Form 413 may be used for this purpose) for each stockholder (with 20% or greater ownership), partner, officer, and owner. Include the assets and liabilities of the spouse and any close relatives living in the household. Also, include your Social Security Number. The date should be the same as the most recent business financial statement. Label it Exhibit B

4. Include the financial statements listed below: a,b,c for the last three years; also a,b,c, and d as of the same date, - current within 90 days of filing the application; and statement e, if applicable. Label it Exhibit C (Contact SBA for referral if assistance with preparation is wanted.) All information must be signed and dated.
 a. Balance Sheet
 b. Profit and Loss Statement (if not available, explain why and substitute Federal income tax forms)
 c. Reconciliation of Net Worth
 d. Aging of Accounts Receivable and Payable (summary not detailed)
 e. Projection of earnings for at least one year where financial statements for the last three years are unavailable or when

5. Provide a brief history of your company and a paragraph describing the expected benefits it will receive from the loan. Label it Exhibit D.

6. Provide a brief description similar to a resume of the education, technical and business background for all the people listed under Management. Label it Exhibit E.

ALL EXHIBITS MUST BE SIGNED AND DATED BY PERSON SIGNING THIS FORM

7. Submit the names, addresses, tax I.D. number(EIN or SSN), and current personal balance sheet(s) of any co-signers and/or guarantors for the loan who are not otherwise affiliated with the business as Exhibit F.

8. Include a list of any machinery or equipment or other non-real estate assets to be purchased with loan proceeds and the cost of each item as quoted by the seller as Exhibit G. Include the seller's name and address.

9. Have you or any officers of your company ever been involved in bankruptcy or insolvency proceedings? If so, please provide the details as Exhibit H.
If none, check here: [ ]Yes [ ]No

10. Are you or your business involved in any pending lawsuits? If yes, provide the details as Exhibit I.
If none, check here: [ ]Yes [ ]No

11. Do you or your spouse or any member of your household, or anyone who owns, manages or directs your business or their spouses or members of their households work for the Small Business Administration, Small Business Advisory Council, SCORE or ACE, any Federal Agency, or the participating lender? If so, please provide the name and address of the person and the office where employed.) Label this Exhibit J.
If none, check here:

12. Does your business, its owners or majority stockholders own or have a controlling interest in other businesses? If yes, please provide their names and the relationship with your company along with a current balance sheet and operating statement for each. This should be Exhibit K.

13. Do you buy from, sell to, or use the services of any concern in which someone in your company has a significant financial interest? If yes, provide details on a separate sheet of paper labeled Exhibit L.

14. If your business is a franchise, include a copy of the franchise agreement and a copy of the FTC disclosure statement supplied to you by the Franchisor. Please include it as Exhibit M.

CONSTRUCTION LOANS ONLY

15. Include as a separate exhibit (Exhibit N) the estimated cost of the project and a statement of the source of any additional funds.

16. Provide copies of preliminary construction plans and specifications. Include them as Exhibit O. Final plans will be required prior to disbursement

EXPORT LOANS

17. Does your business presently engage in Export Trade?
Check here: [ ]Yes [ ]No

18. Will you be using proceeds from this loan to support your company's exports?
Check here: [ ]Yes [ ]No

19. Would you like information on Exporting?
Check here: [ ]Yes [ ]No

AGREEMENTS AND CERTIFICATIONS

Agreements of non-employment of SBA Personnel: I agree that if SBA approves this loan application I will not, for at least two years, hire as an employee or consultant anyone that was employed by SBA during the one year period prior to the disbursement of the .

Certification: I certify: (a) I have not paid anyone connected with the Federal Government for help in getting this loan. I also agree to report to the SBA office of the Inspector General, Washington, DC 20416 any Federal Government employee who offers, in return for any type of compensation, to help get this loan approved.

(b) All information in this application and the Exhibits are true and complete to the best of my knowledge and are submitted to SBA so SBA can decide whether to grant a loan or participate with a lending institution in a loan to me. I agree to pay for or reimburse SBA for the cost of any surveys, title or mortgage examinations, appraisals, credit reports, etc., performed by non-SBA personnel provided I

(c) I understand that I need not pay anybody to deal with SBA. I have read and understand SBA Form 159, which explains SBA policy on representatives and their fees .

(d) As consideration for any Management, Technical, and Business Development Assistance that may be provided, I waive all claims against SBA and its consultants.

If you knowingly make a false statement or overvalue a security to obtain a guaranteed loan from SBA, you can be fined up to $10,000 and/or imprisoned for not more than five years under 18 usc 1001; if submitted to a Federally insured institution, under 18 USC 1014 by imprisonment of not more than twenty years and/or a fine of not more than $1,000,000. I authorize the SBA's Office of Inspector General to request criminal record information about me from criminal justice agencies for the purpose of determining my eligibility for programs authorized by

If Applicant is a proprietor or general partner, sign below:

By: _____

If Applicant is a Corporation, sign below:

Corporate Name and Seal   Date
_____

By: _____
           Signature of President

Attested by:_____
          Signature of Corporate Secretary

SUBMIT COMPLETED APPLICATION TO LENDER OF CHOICE

SBA Form 4 (3-00)Previous Edition Obsolete

Page 3

SBA FORM 4—APPLICATION FOR BUSINESS LOAN

APPLICANT'S CERTIFICATION

By my signature, I certify that I have read and received a copy of the "STATEMENTS REQUIRED BY LAW AND EXECUTIVE ORDER" which was attached to this application. My signature represents my agreement to comply with the approval of my loan request and to comply, whenever applicable, with the hazard insurance, lead-based paint, civil rights or other limitations in this notice.

Each proprietor, each General Partner, each Limited Partner or Stockholder owning 20% or more, each Guarantor and the spouse of each of these must sign. Each person should sign only once

Business Name: _____

By: _____   Date _____
   Signature and Title

Guarantors:

_____   Date _____
Signature and Title

_____   Date _____
Signature and Title

_____   Date _____
Signature and Title

_____   Date _____
Signature and Title

_____   Date _____
Signature and Title

_____   Date _____
Signature and Title

_____   Date _____
Signature and Title

SBA Form 4 (3-00)Previous Edition Obsolete

Page 4

PLEASE READ DETACH AND RETAIN FOR YOUR RECORDS
STATEMENTS REQUIRED BY LAW AND EXECUTIVE ORDER

Federal executive agencies, including the Small Business Administration (SBA), are required to withhold or limit financial assistance, to impose special conditions on approved loans, to provide special notices to applicants or borrowers and to require special reports and data from borrowers in order to comply with legislation passed by the Congress and Executive Orders issued by the President and by the provisions of various inter-agency agreements. SBA has issued regulations and procedures that implement these laws and executive orders, and they are contained in Parts 112, 113, 116, and 117, Title 13, Code of Federal Regulations Chapter 1, or Standard Operating Procedures.

Freedom of Information Act (5 U.S.C. 552)
This law provides, with some exceptions, that SBA must supply information reflected in agency files and records to a person requesting it. Information about approved loans that will be automatically released includes, among other things, statistics on our loan programs (individual borrowers are not identified in the statistics) and other information such as the names of the borrowers (and their officers, directors, stockholders or partners), the collateral pledged to secure the loan, the amount of the loan, its purpose in general terms and the maturity. Proprietary data on a borrower would not routinely be made available to third parties. All requests under this Act are to be addressed to the nearest SBA office and be identified as a Freedom of Information request.

Right to Financial Privacy Act of 1978 (12 U.S.C. 3401)
This is notice to you as required by the Right of Financial Privacy Act of 1978, of SBA's access rights to financial records held by financial institutions that are or have been doing business with you or your business, including any financial institutions participating in a loan or loan guarantee. The law provides that SBA shall have a right of access to your financial records in connection with its consideration or administration of assistance to you in the form of a Government loan or loan guaranty agreement. SBA is required to provide a certificate of its compliance with the Act to a financial institution in connection with its first request for access to your financial records, after which no further certification is required for subsequent accesses. The law also provides that SBA's access rights continue for the term of any approved loan or loan guaranty agreement. No further notice to you of SBA's access rights is required during the term of any such agreement.

The law also authorizes SBA to transfer to another Government authority any financial records included in an application for a loan, or concerning an approved loan or loan guarantee, as necessary to process, service or foreclose on a loan or loan guarantee or to collect on a defaulted loan or loan guarantee. No other transfer of your financial records to another Government authority will be permitted by SBA except as required or permitted by law.

Flood Disaster Protection Act (42 U.S.C. 4011)
Regulations have been issued by the Federal Insurance Administration (FIA) and by SBA implementing this Act and its amendments. These regulations prohibit SBA from making certain loans in an FIA designated floodplain unless Federal flood insurance is purchased as a condition of the loan. Failure to maintain the required level of flood insurance makes the applicant ineligible for any future financial assistance from SBA under any program, including disaster assistance.

Executive Orders -- Floodplain Management and Wetland Protection (42 F.R. 26951 and 42 F.R. 26961)
The SBA discourages any settlement in or development of a floodplain or a wetland. This statement is to notify all SBA loan applicants that such actions are hazardous to both life and property and should be avoided. The additional cost of flood preventive construction must be considered in addition to the possible loss of all assets and investments in future floods.

Occupational Safety and Health Act (15 U.S.C. 651 et seq.)
This legislation authorizes the Occupational Safety and Health Administration in the Department of Labor to require businesses to modify facilities and procedures to protect employees or pay penalty fees. In some instances the business can be forced to cease operations or be prevented from starting operations in a new facility. Therefore, in some instances SBA may require additional information from an applicant to determine whether the business will be in compliance with OSHA regulations and allowed to operate its facility after the loan is approved and disbursed.

Signing this form as borrower is a certification that the OSA requirements that apply to the borrower's business have been determined and the borrower to the best of its knowledge is in compliance.

Civil Rights Legislation
All businesses receiving SBA financial assistance must agree not to discriminate in any business practice, including employment practices and services to the public, on the basis of categories cited in 13 C.F.R., Parts 112, 113, and 117 of SBA Regulations. This includes making their goods and services available to handicapped clients or customers. All business borrowers will be required to display the "Equal Employment Opportunity Poster" prescribed by SBA.

Equal Credit Opportunity Act (15 U.S.C. 1691)
The Federal Equal Credit Opportunity Act prohibits creditors from discriminating against credit applicants on the basis of race, color, religion, national origin, sex, marital status or age (provided that the applicant has the capacity to enter into a binding contract); because all or part of the applicant's income derives from any public assistance program, or because the applicant has in good faith exercised any right under the Consumer Credit Protection Act. The Federal agency that administers compliance with this law concerning this creditor is the Federal Trade Commission, Equal Credit Opportunity, Washington, D.C. 20580.

Executive Order 11738 -- Environmental Protection (38 C.F.R. 25161)
The Executive Order charges SBA with administering its loan programs in a manner that will result in effective enforcement of the Clean Air Act, the Federal Water Pollution Act and other environmental protection legislation. SBA must, therefore, impose conditions on some loans. By acknowledging receipt of this form and presenting the application, the principals of all small businesses borrowing $100,000 or more in direct funds stipulate to the following:

1. That any facility used, or to be used, by the subject firm is not cited on the EPA list of Violating Facilities.

2. That subject firm will comply with all the requirements of Section 114 of the Clean Air Act (42 U.S.C. 7414) and Section 308 of the Water Act (33 U.S.C 1318) relating to inspection, monitoring, entry, reports and information, as well as all other requirements specified in Section 114 and Section 308 of the respective Acts, and all regulations and guidelines issued thereunder.

3. That subject firm will notify SBA of the receipt of any communication from the Director of the Environmental Protection Agency indicating that a facility utilized, or to be utilized, by subject firm is under consideration to be listed on the EPA List of Violating Facilities.

Debt Collection Act of 1982 Deficit Reduction Act of 1984 (31 U.S.C. 3701 et seq. and other titles)
These laws require SBA to aggressively collect any loan payments which become delinquent. SBA must obtain your taxpayer identification number when you apply for a loan. If you receive a loan, and do not make payments as they come due, SBA may take one or more of the following actions:

- Report the status of your loan(s) to credit bureaus
- Hire a collection agency to collect your loan
- Offset your income tax refund or other amounts due to you from the Federal Government
- Suspend or debar you or your company from doing business with the Federal Government
- Refer your loan to the Department of Justice or other attorneys for litigation
- Foreclose on collateral or take other action permitted in the loan instruments.

Immigration Reform and Control Act of 1986 (Pub. L. 99-603)
If you are an alien who was in this country illegally since before January 1, 1982, you may have been granted lawful temporary resident status by the United States Immigration and Naturalization Service pursuant to the Immigration Reform and Control Act of 1986 (Pub. L. 99-603). For five years from the date you are granted such status, you are not eligible for financial assistance from the SBA in the form of a loan or guaranty under section 7(a) of the Small Business Act unless you are disabled or a Cuban or Haitian entrant. When you sign this document, you are making the certification that the Immigration Reform and Control Act of 1986 does not apply to you, or if it does apply, more than five years have elapsed since you have been granted lawful temporary resident status pursuant to such 1986 legislation.

Lead-Based Paint Poisoning Prevention Act (42 U.S.C. 4821 et seq.)
Borrowers using SBA funds for the construction or rehabilitation of a residential structure are prohibited from using lead-based paint (as defined in SBA regulations) on all interior surfaces, whether accessible or not, and exterior surfaces, such as stairs, decks, porches, railings, windows and doors, which are readily accessible to children under 7 years of age. A "residential structure" is any home, apartment, hotel, motel, orphanage, boarding school, dormitory, day care center, extended care facility, college or other school housing, hospital, group practice or community facility and all other residential or institutional structures where persons reside.

APPENDIX 14:
EMPLOYMENT AGREEMENT

This Agreement dated July 1, 2001, is by and between ABC COMPANY, 123 Main Street, City, State 00000 (hereinafter Company), and John Smith, 456 Central Avenue, City, State 00000, (hereinafter Employee).

For valuable consideration, Company and Independent Contractor agree as follows:

ARTICLE ONE: TITLE

1. Company hereby engages the services of employee as its (specify title).

ARTICLE TWO: TERM

2. Employee hereby agrees to perform services for Company in the capacity of (title), for a one-year term beginning July 1, 2001 and ending July1, 2003.

3. This agreement may be renewed annually, for one additional year, on the same terms and conditions as contained herein, unless either party notifies the other prior to the end of the existing term, of that party's intention not to renew this agreement.

ARTICLE THREE: COMPENSATION

4. Company agrees to compensate employee as follows:

a) For the first year during which this agreement is in effect, Company agrees to compensate employee for services rendered at an annual salary of $ _____ .

b) For the second year, and all succeeding years, during which this agreement is in effect, the employee shall receive an increase to employee's then annual salary of twenty percent (20%).

c) In addition to employee's annual salary, employee will be entitled to an annual bonus equal to ten percent (10%) of employees then annual salary.

ARTICLE FOUR: JOB DESCRIPTION

5. Employee shall perform the following duties and responsibilities: (Specify duties and responsibilities)

ARTICLE FIVE: PERFORMANCE EVALUATION

6. Employee's performance will be evaluated by management on an annual basis to determine whether employee's contract shall be renewed for an additional 1-year term. Such evaluation shall take place prior to the expiration to the existing term.

ARTICLE SIX: EMPLOYEE EXPENSE ACCOUNT

7. Company shall pay or reimburse employee for all ordinary and necessary expenses incurred by employee in performance of his or her duties under this agreement, upon submission by employee of the appropriate expense account forms.

ARTICLE SEVEN: INSURANCE

8. Company shall purchase a term life plan insurance policy on the life of the employee in a policy amount of not less than [Insert $ Amount], and shall pay all premiums due and owing on such policy. The employee shall designate the beneficiary to such policy.

9. Company shall provide employee with medical and hospital insurance as outlined in Company's employee handbook, a copy of which is attached hereto.

ARTICLE EIGHT: VACATION AND PERSONAL LEAVE

10. Employee shall be entitled to accrue vacation and personal leave time as outlined in Company's employee handbook, a copy of which is attached hereto.

ARTICLE NINE: NOTICES

11. Any notice required to be given under this agreement shall be sent by certified mail, return receipt requested, as follows:

To Company:

ABC Company
123 Main Street
City, State 00000

To Employee:

John Smith
456 Central Avenue
City, State 00000

ARTICLE TEN: ADDITIONAL PROVISIONS

12. The waiver by either party of any term or condition of this agreement shall not constitute a waiver of any other term or condition of this agreement.

13. This agreement contains the entire understanding of the partners.

14. Any modification of this agreement must be in writing and signed by both parties.

15. This Agreement is being made in [Name of State] and shall be construed and enforced according to the laws of that state.

16. Additional Terms (specify):

IN WITNESS WHEREOF, the parties have duly executed this Agreement as of the date first written above.

Signature Line for Employer ABC Company

Signature Line for Employee John Smith

APPENDIX 15:
FORM I-9—INS EMPLOYMENT ELIGIBILITY VERIFICATION FORM

U.S. Department of Justice
Immigration and Naturalization Service

OMB No. 1115-0136

Employment Eligibility Verification

INSTRUCTIONS
PLEASE READ ALL INSTRUCTIONS CAREFULLY BEFORE COMPLETING THIS FORM.

Anti-Discrimination Notice. It is illegal to discriminate against any individual (other than an alien not authorized to work in the U.S.) in hiring, discharging, or recruiting or referring for a fee because of that individual's national origin or citizenship status. It is illegal to discriminate against work eligible individuals. Employers **CANNOT** specify which document(s) they will accept from an employee. The refusal to hire an individual because of a future expiration date may also constitute illegal discrimination.

Section 1 - Employee. All employees, citizens and noncitizens, hired after November 6, 1986, must complete Section 1 of this form at the time of hire, which is the actual beginning of employment. **The employer is responsible for ensuring that Section 1 is timely and properly completed.**

Preparer/Translator Certification. The Preparer/Translator Certification must be completed if Section 1 is prepared by a person other than the employee. A preparer/translator may be used only when the employee is unable to complete Section 1 on his/her own. However, the employee must still sign Section 1.

Section 2 - Employer. For the purpose of completing this form, the term "employer" includes those recruiters and referrers for a fee who are agricultural associations, agricultural employers or farm labor contractors.

Employers must complete Section 2 by examining evidence of identity and employment eligibility within three (3) business days of the date employment begins. If employees are authorized to work, but are unable to present the required document(s) within three business days, they must present a receipt for the application of the document(s) within three business days and the actual document(s) within ninety (90) days. However, if employers hire individuals for a duration of less than three business days, Section 2 must be completed at the time employment begins. **Employers must record: 1)** document title; **2)** issuing authority; **3)** document number, **4)** expiration date, if any; and **5)** the date employment begins. Employers must sign and date the certification. Employees must present original documents. Employers may, but are not required to, photocopy the document(s) presented. These photocopies may only be used for the verification process and must be retained with the I-9. **However, employers are still responsible for completing the I-9.**

Section 3 - Updating and Reverification. Employers must complete Section 3 when updating and/or reverifying the I-9. Employers must reverify employment eligibility of their employees on or before the expiration date recorded in Section 1. Employers **CANNOT** specify which document(s) they will accept from an employee.

- If an employee's name has changed at the time this form is being updated/ reverified, complete Block A.

- If an employee is rehired within three (3) years of the date this form was originally completed and the employee is still eligible to be employed on the same basis as previously indicated on this form (updating), complete Block B and the signature block.

- If an employee is rehired within three (3) years of the date this form was originally completed and the employee's work authorization has expired or if a current employee's work authorization is about to expire (reverification), complete Block B and:
  - examine any document that reflects that the employee is authorized to work in the U.S. (see List A or C),
  - record the document title, document number and expiration date (if any) in Block C, and complete the signature block.

Photocopying and Retaining Form I-9. A blank I-9 may be reproduced, provided both sides are copied. The Instructions must be available to all persons completing this form. Employers must retain completed I-9s for three (3) years after the date of hire or one (1) year after the date employment ends, whichever is later.

For more detailed information, you may refer to the INS Handbook for Employers, (Form M-274). You may obtain the handbook at your local INS office.

Privacy Act Notice. The authority for collecting this information is the Immigration Reform and Control Act of 1986, Pub. L. 99-603 (8 USC 1324a).

This information is for employers to verify the eligibility of individuals for employment to preclude the unlawful hiring, or recruiting or referring for a fee, of aliens who are not authorized to work in the United States.

This information will be used by employers as a record of their basis for determining eligibility of an employee to work in the United States. The form will be kept by the employer and made available for inspection by officials of the U.S. Immigration and Naturalization Service, the Department of Labor and the Office of Special Counsel for Immigration Related Unfair Employment Practices.

Submission of the information required in this form is voluntary. However, an individual may not begin employment unless this form is completed, since employers are subject to civil or criminal penalties if they do not comply with the Immigration Reform and Control Act of 1986.

Reporting Burden. We try to create forms and instructions that are accurate, can be easily understood and which impose the least possible burden on you to provide us with information. Often this is difficult because some immigration laws are very complex. Accordingly, the reporting burden for this collection of information is computed as follows: **1)** learning about this form, 5 minutes; **2)** completing the form, 5 minutes; and **3)** assembling and filing (recordkeeping) the form, 5 minutes, for an average of 15 minutes per response. If you have comments regarding the accuracy of this burden estimate, or suggestions for making this form simpler, you can write to the Immigration and Naturalization Service, HQPDI, 425 I Street, N.W., Room 4307r, Washington, DC 20536. OMB No. 1115-0136.

EMPLOYERS MUST RETAIN COMPLETED FORM I-9
PLEASE DO NOT MAIL COMPLETED FORM I-9 TO INS

Form I-9 (Rev. 11-21-91)N

U.S. Department of Justice
Immigration and Naturalization Service

OMB No. 1115-0136

Employment Eligibility Verification

Please read instructions carefully before completing this form. The instructions must be available during completion of this form. **ANTI-DISCRIMINATION NOTICE:** It is illegal to discriminate against work eligible individuals. Employers CANNOT specify which document(s) they will accept from an employee. The refusal to hire an individual because of a future expiration date may also constitute illegal discrimination.

Section 1. Employee Information and Verification. To be completed and signed by employee at the time employment begins.

Print Name: Last	First	Middle Initial	Maiden Name

Address (Street Name and Number)		Apt. #	Date of Birth (month/day/year)

City	State	Zip Code	Social Security #

I am aware that federal law provides for imprisonment and/or fines for false statements or use of false documents in connection with the completion of this form.	I attest, under penalty of perjury, that I am (check one of the following): ☐ A citizen or national of the United States ☐ A Lawful Permanent Resident (Alien # A_____) ☐ An alien authorized to work until __/__/__ (Alien # or Admission #) _____
Employee's Signature	Date (month/day/year)

Preparer and/or Translator Certification. (To be completed and signed if Section 1 is prepared by a person other than the employee.) I attest, under penalty of perjury, that I have assisted in the completion of this form and that to the best of my knowledge the information is true and correct.

Preparer's/Translator's Signature	Print Name
Address (Street Name and Number, City, State, Zip Code)	Date (month/day/year)

Section 2. Employer Review and Verification. To be completed and signed by employer. Examine one document from List A OR examine one document from List B and one from List C, as listed on the reverse of this form, and record the title, number and expiration date, if any, of the document(s)

	List A	OR	List B	AND	List C
Document title:					
Issuing authority:					
Document #:					
Expiration Date (if any):	__/__/__		__/__/__		__/__/__
Document #:					
Expiration Date (if any):	__/__/__				

CERTIFICATION - I attest, under penalty of perjury, that I have examined the document(s) presented by the above-named employee, that the above-listed document(s) appear to be genuine and to relate to the employee named, that the employee began employment on (month/day/year) __/__/__ and that to the best of my knowledge the employee is eligible to work in the United States. (State employment agencies may omit the date the employee began employment.)

Signature of Employer or Authorized Representative	Print Name	Title
Business or Organization Name	Address (Street Name and Number, City, State, Zip Code)	Date (month/day/year)

Section 3. Updating and Reverification. To be completed and signed by employer.

A. New Name (if applicable)	B. Date of rehire (month/day/year) (if applicable)

C. If employee's previous grant of work authorization has expired, provide the information below for the document that establishes current employment eligibility.

Document Title:_____   Document #:_____   Expiration Date (if any): __/__/__

I attest, under penalty of perjury, that to the best of my knowledge, this employee is eligible to work in the United States, and if the employee presented document(s), the document(s) I have examined appear to be genuine and to relate to the individual.

Signature of Employer or Authorized Representative	Date (month/day/year)

Form I-9 (Rev. 11-21-91)N Page 2

APPENDIX 16:
LIST OF ACCEPTABLE EMPLOYEE IDENTIFICATION DOCUMENTS

The following is a partial list of valid documents from which the employee may choose to present proof of identity to his or her employer in conjunction with the completion of INS Form I-9. The employee may choose one document from LIST A. Or, the employee may choose two documents, one from LIST B, that shows identity and one from LIST C that shows work authorization.

LIST A—DOCUMENTS THAT ESTABLISH BOTH IDENTITY AND EMPLOYMENT ELIGIBILITY

1. U.S. Passport (unexpired or expired)

2. Certificate of U.S. Citizenship (INS Form N-560 or N-561)

3. Certificate of Naturalization (INS Form N-550 or N-570)

4. Unexpired Foreign Passport (with I-551 stamp or attached INS Form I-94 indicating unexpired employment authorization)

5. Alien Registration Receipt Card with Photograph (INS Form I or I-551)

6. Unexpired Temporary Resident Card (INS Form I-688)

7. Unexpired Employment Authorization Card (INS Form I-688A)

8. Unexpired Reentry Permit (INS Form I-327)

9. Unexpired Refugee Travel Document (INS Form I-571)

10. Unexpired Employment Authorization Document Issued by the INS with Photograph (INS form I-688B)

LIST B—DOCUMENTS THAT ESTABLISH IDENTITY

1. Driver's License or ID Card Issued by a State or Outlying Possession of the United States (provided it contains a photograph or information such as name, date of birth, sex, height, eye color and address)

2. ID Card Issued by Federal, State or Local Government Agencies or Entities (provided it contains a photograph or information such as name, date of birth, sex, height, eye color and address)

3. School ID Cared with Photograph

4. Voter Registration Card

5. U.S. Military Card or Draft Record

6. Military Dependent's ID Card

7. U.S. Coast Guard Merchant Mariner Card

8. Native American Tribal Document

9. Driver's License Issued by a Canadian Government Authority

FOR PERSONS UNDER AGE 18 WHO ARE UNABLE TO PRESENT A DOCUMENT LISTED ABOVE:

10. School Record or Report Card

11. Clinic, Doctor or Hospital Record

12. Day Care or Nursery School Record

LIST C—DOCUMENTS THAT ESTABLISH EMPLOYMENT ELIGIBILITY

1. U.S. Social Security Card Issued by the Social Security Administration (other than a card stating it is not valid for employment)

2. Certification of Birth Abroad Issued by the Department of State (Form FS-545 or Form DS-1350)

3. Original or Certified Copy of a Birth Certificate Issued by a State, County, Municipal Authority or Outlying Possession of the United States Bearing an Official Seal

4. Native American Tribal Document

5. U.S. Citizen ID Card (INS Form I-197)

6. ID Card for Use of Resident Citizen in the United States (INS Form I-179)

7. Unexpired Employment Authorization Document Issued by the INS (other than those listed under List A)

APPENDIX 17:
INDEPENDENT CONTRACTOR AGREEMENT

This Agreement dated July 1, 2001, is by and between ABC COMPANY, (Company), and John Smith, (Independent Contractor).

For valuable consideration, Company and Independent Contractor agree as follows:

ARTICLE ONE: SERVICES

1. Contractor agrees to perform the following services for Company: (specify)

ARTICLE TWO: COMPLETION

2. Contractor agrees that the services described in Article One will be commenced on July 1, 2001, and will be completed by August 1, 2001.

ARTICLE THREE: LABOR

3. Contractor agrees to hire and compensate Contractor's own employees to perform services under this contract.

ARTICLE FOUR: MATERIALS

4. Contractor agrees to furnish all materials necessary to perform services under this contract.

ARTICLE FIVE: PAYMENT

5. Company agrees to pay Contractor the total amount of [Insert $ Amount] for Contractor's services under this contract. Such payment shall be made as follows: (specify)

ARTICLE SIX: MISCELLANEOUS PROVISIONS

6. The parties agree that Independent Contractor is not an employee of Company and Contractor shall not represent that he or she is an employee of the Company.

7. Contractor agrees to indemnify and hold Company harmless from any claims or liabilities arising out of the performance of Contractor's services under this contract.

8. This agreement contains the entire understanding of the partners.

9. Any modification of this agreement must be in writing and signed by both parties.

10. This Agreement is being made in [Name of State] and shall be construed and enforced according to the laws of that state.

11. Additional Terms (specify):

IN WITNESS WHEREOF, the parties have duly executed this Agreement as of the date first written above.

Signature Line for ABC Company

Signature Line for Independent Contractor John Smith

APPENDIX 18:
REGIONAL DIRECTORY OF OCCUPATIONAL
SAFETY AND HEALTH ADMINISTRATION
OFFICES

REGION	TELEPHONE NUMBER
ATLANTA, GEORGIA	404-347-3573
BOSTON, MASSACHUSETTS	617-565-7164
CHICAGO, ILLINOIS	312-353-2220
DALLAS, TEXAS	214-767-4731
DENVER, COLORADO	303-844-3061
KANSAS CITY, MISSOURI	816-426-5681
NEW YORK, NEW YORK	212-337-2378
PHILADELPHIA, PENNSYLVANIA	215-596-1201
SAN FRANCISCO, CALIFORNIA	415-744-6670
SEATTLE, WASHINGTON	206-442-5930

GLOSSARY

ACCOUNTS PAYABLE—Trade accounts of businesses representing obligations to pay for goods and services received.

ACCOUNTS RECEIVABLE—Trade accounts of businesses representing moneys due for goods sold or services rendered evidenced by notes, statements, invoices or other written evidence of a present obligation.

ACCOUNTING—The recording, classifying, summarizing and interpreting in a significant manner and in terms of money, transactions and events of a financial character.

ADHESION CONTRACT—A standardized contract form offered to consumers of goods and services on a "take it or leave it" basis without affording the consumer a realistic opportunity to bargain, and under such conditions that infer coercion.

AGENCY—The relationship between a principal and an agent who is employed by the principal, to perform certain acts dealing with third parties.

AGENT—One who represents another known as the principal.

ANTITRUST LAWS—Statutes designed to promote free competition in the market place.

APPARENT AGENCY—Apparent agency exists when one person, whether or not authorized, reasonably appears to a third person to be authorized to act as agent for such other.

ARBITRATION—The reference of a dispute to an impartial person chosen by the parties to the dispute who agree in advance to abide by the arbitrator's award issued after a hearing at which both parties have an opportunity to be heard.

ARBITRATION ACTS—Federal and state laws which provide for submission of disputes to the process of arbitration.

ARBITRATION BOARD—A panel of arbitrators appointed to hear and decide a dispute according to the rules of arbitration.

ARBITRATION CLAUSE—A clause inserted in a contract providing for compulsory arbitration in case of a dispute as to the rights or liabilities under such contract.

ARBITRATOR—A private, disinterested person, chosen by the parties to a disputed question, for the purpose of hearing their contention, and awarding judgment to the prevailing party.

ARM'S LENGTH—Refers to the bargaining position of two parties that are unrelated to one another and have no other motivation for dealing other than to transact business in good faith.

ASSUMPTION—The act of assuming/undertaking another's debts or obligations.

AUCTION—A public sale of goods to the highest bidder.

AUTOMATIC DATA PROCESSING—Data processing largely performed by automatic means.

BALANCE SHEET—A report of the status of a firm's assets, liabilities and owner's equity at a given time.

BAD FAITH—A willful failure to comply with one's statutory or contractual obligations.

BANKRUPTCY—A condition in which a business cannot meet its debt obligations and petitions a federal district court for either reorganization of its debts or liquidation of its assets.

BID—An offer to buy goods or services at a stated price.

BILATERAL CONTRACT—A bilateral contract is one containing mutual promises between the parties to the contract, each being termed both a promisor and a promisee.

BILL—In commercial law, an account for goods sold, services rendered and work done.

BILL OF LADING—In commercial law, the document given to the shipper by the carrier in connection with goods to be transported by the carrier.

BILL OF SALE—A written agreement by which the exchange of personal property is made.

BOARD OF DIRECTORS—The governing body of a corporation which is elected by the stockholders.

BOILERPLATE—Refers to standard language found almost universally in certain documents.

BREACH OF CONTRACT—The failure, without any legal excuse, to perform any promise which forms the whole or the part of a contract.

BREACH OF WARRANTY—An infraction of an express or implied agreement as to the title, quality, content or condition of a thing which is sold.

BREAK-EVEN POINT—The break-even point in any business is that point at which the volume of sales or revenues exactly equals total expenses —i.e., the point at which there is neither a profit nor loss.

BULK SALES ACT—Statutes designed to prevent the defrauding of a merchant's creditors by the secret bulk sale of substantially all of the merchant's stock.

BULK TRANSFER—A type of commercial fraud wherein a merchant transfers all or most of the business, for consideration, without paying creditors from the proceeds of the sale.

BUSINESS BIRTH—Formation of a new establishment or enterprise.

BUSINESS DEATH—Voluntary or involuntary closure of a firm or establishment.

BUSINESS DISSOLUTION—For enumeration purposes, the absence from any current record of a business that was present in a prior time period.

BUSINESS FAILURE —The closure of a business causing a loss to at least one creditor.

BUSINESS INFORMATION CENTER (BIC)—One of more than 50 specialized Small Business Administration units which offer the latest in high-technology hard-ware, software and telecommunications to assist small business and one-on-one counseling with seasoned business veterans through the Service Corps of Retired Executives (SCORE).

BUSINESS PLAN—A comprehensive planning document which clearly describes the business developmental objective of an existing or proposed business and outlines what and how and from where the resources needed to accomplish the objective will be obtained and utilized.

BUSINESS START—For enumeration purposes, a business with a name or similar designation that did not exist in a prior time period.

CANCELED LOAN—The annulment or rescission of an approved loan prior to disbursement.

CAPITAL—Assets less liabilities, representing the ownership interest in a business.

CAPITAL CONTRIBUTION—Cash, property or services contributed by partners to a partnership.

CAPITAL EXPENDITURES—Business spending on additional equipment and inventory.

CAPITAL GAIN—The excess of proceeds over cost, or other basis, from the sale of a capital asset.

CAPITAL LOSS—Loss on the sale or exchange of a capital asset.

CAPITALIZED PROPERTY—Personal property of the business which has an average dollar value of $300.00 or more and a life expectancy of one year or more.

CASH DISCOUNT—An incentive offered by the seller to encourage the buyer to pay within a stipulated time.

CASH FLOW—The amount of funds a business receives during any given period minus what is paid out during the same period.

CHARGE-OFF—An accounting transaction removing an uncollectible balance from the active receivable accounts.

CHARGED OFF LOAN—An uncollectible loan for which the principal and accrued interest were removed from the receivable accounts.

CHARTER—The document issued by the government establishing a corporate entity.

CLAYTON ACT—A federal statute amending the Sherman Antitrust Act.

CLOSE CORPORATION—A corporation whose shares, or at least voting shares, are held by a single shareholder or closely-knit group of shareholders.

CLOSED LOAN—Any loan for which funds have been disbursed, and all required documentation has been executed, received and reviewed.

CLOSING—Actions and procedures required to effect the documentation and disbursement of loan funds after the application has been approved, and the execution of all required documentation and its filing and recordation where required.

COLLATERAL—Something of value—securities, evidence of deposit or other property—pledged to support the repayment of an obligation.

COLLATERAL DOCUMENT—A legal document covering the item(s) pledged as collateral on a loan, i.e., note, mortgages, assignment, etc.

COMMINGLE—To combine funds or properties into a common fund.

COMPROMISE—The settlement of a claim resulting from a defaulted loan for less than the full amount due.

COMPULSORY ARBITRATION—Arbitration which occurs when the consent of one of the parties is enforced by statutory provisions.

CONSOLIDATION—A combination of two or more corporations which are succeeded by a new corporation, usually with a new title.

CONSORTIUM—A coalition of organizations, such as banks and corporations, set up to fund ventures requiring large capital resources.

CONSUMER CREDIT—Loans and sale credit extended to individuals to finance the purchases of goods and services arising out of consumer needs and desires.

CONTINGENT LIABILITY—A potential obligation that may be incurred dependent upon the occurrence of a future event.

CONTRACT—A contract is an agreement between two or more persons which creates an obligation to do or not to do a particular thing.

CORPORATION—A group of persons granted a state charter legally recognizing them as a separate entity having its own rights, privileges, and liabilities distinct from those of its members.

COSTS—Money obligated for goods and services received during a given period of time, regardless of when ordered or whether paid for.

CREDIT RATING—A grade assigned to a business concern to denote the net worth and credit standing to which the concern is entitled in the opinion of the rating agency as a result of its investigation.

DEBENTURE—Debt instrument evidencing the holder's right to receive interest and principal installments from the named obligor.

DEBT CAPITAL—Business financing that normally requires periodic interest payments and repayment of the principal within a specified time.

DEBT FINANCING—The provision of long term loans to small business concerns in exchange for debt securities or a note.

DEED OF TRUST—A document under seal which, when delivered, transfers a present interest in property and may be held as collateral.

DEFAULTS—The nonpayment of principal and/or interest on the due date as provided by the terms and conditions of the note.

DEFERRED LOAN—Loans whose principal and or interest installments are postponed for a specified period of time.

DEMAND FOR ARBITRATION—A unilateral filing of a claim in arbitration based on the filer's contractual or statutory right to do so.

DISCLAIMER—Words or conduct which tend to negate or limit warranty in the sale of goods, which in certain instances must be conspicuous and refer to the specific warranty to be excluded.

DIVESTITURE—Change of ownership and/or control of a business from a majority to disadvantaged persons.

DOMESTIC CORPORATION—In reference to a particular state, a domestic corporation is one created by, or organized under, the laws of that state.

DRAM SHOP ACT—Refers to laws which impose strict liability upon the seller of intoxicating beverages when harm is caused to a third party as a result of the sale.

EARNING POWER—The demonstrated ability of a business to earn a profit, over time, while following good accounting practices.

ENTERPRISE—Aggregation of all establishments owned by a parent company, which may consist of a single, independent establishment or subsidiaries or other branch establishments under the same ownership and control.

ENTREPRENEUR—One who assumes the financial risk of the initiation, operation and management of a given business or undertaking.

EQUITY—An ownership interest in a business.

EQUITY FINANCING—The provision of funds for capital or operating expenses in exchange for capital stock, stock purchase warrants and options in the business financed, without any guaranteed return, but with the opportunity to share in the company's profits.

EQUITY PARTNERSHIP—A limited partnership arrangement for providing start-up and seed capital to businesses.

ESCROW ACCOUNT—Funds placed in trust with a third party, by a borrower for a specific purpose and to be delivered to the borrower only upon the fulfillment of certain conditions.

ESTABLISHMENT—A single-location business unit, which may be independent—called a single-establishment enterprise— or owned by a parent enterprise.

FACTORING—A method of financing accounts receivable wherein a firm sells its accounts receivable to a financial institution.

FEATHERBEDDING—An unfair labor practice whereby the time spent, or number of employees needed, to complete a particular task, is increased unnecessarily for the purpose of creating employment.

FEDERAL TRADE COMMISSION—The Federal Trade Commission is an agency of the federal government created in 1914 for the purpose of promoting free and fair competition in interstate commerce through the prevention of general trade restraints.

FINANCE CHARGE—Any charge for an extension of credit, such as interest.

FINANCIAL REPORTS—Reports commonly required from applicants who request financial assistance such as balance sheets, income statements and cash flow charts.

FINANCING—New funds provided to a business, by either loans or purchase of debt securities or capital stock.

FISCAL YEAR—Any twelve-month period used by a business as its fiscal accounting period.

FIXED CAPITAL—The amount of money permanently invested in a business.

FLOW CHART—A graphical representation for the definition, analysis, or solution of a problem, in which symbols are used to represent operations, data, flow, equipment, etc.

FORCE MAJEURE—Force majeure is a clause commonly found in construction contracts which protects the parties in the event that a part of the contract cannot be performed due to causes which are outside the control of the parties.

FORECLOSURE—The act by the mortgagee or trustee upon default, in the payment of interest or principal of a mortgage of enforcing payment of the debt by selling the underlying security.

FOREIGN CORPORATION—In reference to a particular state, a foreign corporation is one created by or under the laws of another state, government or country.

FRANCHISING—A form of business by which the owner—i.e., the franchisor—of a product, service or method obtains distribution through affiliated dealers—i.e., the franchisees—and whereby the product, method or service being marketed is usually identified by the franchisor's brand name, and the franchisee is often given exclusive access to a defined geographical area as well as assistance in organizing, training, merchandising, marketing and managing in return for a consideration.

FREE ON BOARD (FOB)—Free on board is a commercial term that signifies a contractual agreement between a buyer and a seller to have the subject of a sale delivered to a designated place, usually either the place of shipment or the place of destination.

GARNISH—To attach a portion of the wages or other property of a debtor to secure repayment of the debt.

GARNISHEE—A person who receives notice to hold the assets of another, which are in his or her possession, until such time as a court orders the disposition of the property.

GENERAL PARTNER—A partner who participates fully in the profits, losses and management of the partnership, and who is personally liable for its debts.

GENERAL PARTNERSHIP—A type of partnership in which all of the partners share the profits and losses as well as the management fully, though their capital contributions may vary.

GRACE PERIOD—In contract law, a period specified in a contract which is beyond the due date but during which time payment will be accepted without penalty.

GROSS DOMESTIC PRODUCT (GDP)—The most comprehensive single measure of aggregate economic output representing the market value of the total output of the goods and services produced by a nation's economy.

GUARANTEED LOAN—A loan made and serviced by a lending institution under agreement that a governmental agency will purchase the guaranteed portion if the borrower defaults.

HAZARD INSURANCE—Insurance required showing lender as loss payee covering certain risks on real and personal property used for securing loans.

IMPOSSIBILITY—Impossibility is a defense to breach of contract and arises when performance is impossible due to the destruction of the subject matter of the contract or the death of a person necessary for performance.

INCOME STATEMENT—A report of revenue and expenses which shows the results of business operations or net income for a specified period of time.

INCORPORATION—To form a corporation by following established legal procedures.

INDEMNIFICATION CLAUSE—An indemnification clause in a contract refers to the agreement by one party to secure the other party against loss or damage which may occur in the future in connection with performance of the contract.

INDEMNIFY—To hold another harmless for loss or damage which has already occurred, or which may occur in the future.

INDUSTRIAL REVENUE BOND (IRB)—A tax-exempt bond issued by a state or local government agency to finance industrial or commercial projects that serve a public good. The bond usually is not backed by the full faith and credit of the government that issues it, but is repaid solely from the revenues of the project and requires a private sector commitment for repayment.

INNOVATION—Introduction of a new idea into the marketplace in the form of a new product or service, or an improvement in organization or process.

INSOLVENCY—The inability of a borrower to meet financial obligations as they mature, or having insufficient assets to pay legal debts.

INSTALLMENT CONTRACT—An installment contract is one in which the obligation, such as the payment of money, is divided into a series of successive performances over a period of time.

INTEREST—An amount paid a lender for the use of funds.

INVESTMENT BANKING—Businesses specializing in the formation of capital.

JOB DESCRIPTION—A written statement listing the elements of a particular job or occupation, e.g., purpose, duties, equipment used, qualifications, training, physical and mental demands, working conditions, etc.

JUDGMENT—Judicial determination of the existence of an indebtedness, or other legal liability.

JUDGMENT BY CONFESSION—The act of debtors permitting judgment to be entered against them for a given sum with a statement to that effect, without the institution of legal proceedings.

JUDGMENT CREDITOR—A creditor who has obtained a judgment against a debtor, which judgment may be enforced to obtain payment of the amount due.

JUDGMENT DEBTOR—An individual who owes a sum of money, and against whom a judgment has been awarded for that debt.

JUNK BOND—A high-yield corporate bond issue with a below-investment rating that became a growing source of corporate funding in the 1980s.

LABOR ORGANIZATION—An association of workers for the purpose of bargaining the terms and conditions of employment on behalf of labor and management.

LEASE—A contract between an owner—i.e., a lessor—and a tenant—i.e., a lessee—stating the conditions under which the tenant may occupy or use the property.

LEGAL RATE OF INTEREST—The maximum rate of interest fixed by the laws of the various states, which a lender may charge a borrower for the use of money.

LENDING INSTITUTION—Any institution, including a commercial bank, savings and loan association, commercial finance company, or other lender qualified to participate in the making of loans.

LETTER OF INTENT—A non-binding writing intended to set forth the intentions between parties in anticipation of a formal, binding contract.

LEVERAGED BUY-OUT—The purchase of a business, with financing provided largely by borrowed money, often in the form of junk bonds.

LIEN—A charge upon or security interest in real or personal property maintained to ensure the satisfaction of a debt or duty ordinarily arising by operation of law.

LIMITED PARTNER—A partner whose participation in the profits of the business is limited by agreement and who is not liable for the debts of the partnership beyond his or her capital contribution.

LIMITED PARTNERSHIP—A type of partnership comprised of one or more general partners who manage the business and who are personally liable for partnership debts, and one or more limited partners who contribute capital and share in profits but who take no part in running the business and incur no liability with respect to partnership obligations beyond contribution.

LINE OF CREDIT—An arrangement whereby a financial institution commits itself to lend up to a specified maximum amount of funds during a specified period.

LIQUIDATED DAMAGES—An amount stipulated in a contract as a reasonable estimate of damages to be paid in the event the contract is breached.

LIQUIDATION—The disposal, at maximum prices, of the collateral securing a loan, and the voluntary and enforced collection of the remaining loan balance from the obligators and/or guarantors.

LIQUIDATION VALUE—The net value realizable in the sale—ordinarily a forced sale—of a business or a particular asset.

LITIGATION—The practice of taking legal action through the judicial process.

LOAN AGREEMENT—Agreement to be executed by borrower, containing pertinent terms, conditions, covenants and restrictions.

LOAN PAYOFF AMOUNT—The total amount of money needed to meet a borrower's obligation on a loan.

LOSS RATE—A rate developed by comparing the ratio of total loans charged off to the total loans disbursed from inception of the program to the present date.

MARKET—The set of existing and prospective users of a product or service.

MARKET PENETRATION—A systematic campaign to increase sales in current markets of an existing product or service.

MARKET SEGMENT—A distinct or definable subset of a target market.

MARKUP—Markup is the difference between invoice cost and selling price which may be expressed either as a percentage of the selling price or the cost price and is supposed to cover all the costs of doing business plus a profit.

MATERIAL BREACH—A material breach refers to a substantial breach of contract which excuses further performance by the innocent party and gives rise to an action for breach of contract by the injured party.

MATURITY—As applied to securities and commercial paper, the period end date when payment of principal is due.

MATURITY EXTENSIONS—Extensions of payment beyond the original period established for repayment of a loan.

MECHANIC'S LIEN—A claim created by law for the purpose of securing a priority of payment of the price of work performed and materials used.

MERGER—A combination of two or more corporations wherein the dominant unit absorbs the passive ones, and the former continuing operation usually under the same name.

NATIONAL LABOR RELATIONS ACT—A federal statute known as the Wagner Act of 1935 and amended by the Taft-Hartley Act of 1947, w furnished.

MEDIATION—The act of a third person in intermediating between two contending parties with a view to persuading them to adjust or settle their dispute but without the authority to make a binding decision.

MEDIATOR—One who interposes between parties at variance for the purpose of reconciling them.

NATIONAL LABOR RELATIONS BOARD—An independent agency created by the National Labor Relations Act of 1935 (Wagner Act), as amended by the acts of 1947 (Taft-Hartley Act) and 1959 (Landrum-Griffin Act), established to regulate the relations between employers and employees.

NEGOTIATION—In labor law, refers to the "face to face" process used by local unions and the employer to exchange their views on those matters involving personnel policies and practices, or other matters affecting the working conditions of employees.

NEGOTIATION DISPUTE—That point in negotiations where labor and management cannot come to an agreement on some or all of the issues on the bargaining table.

NEGOTIATED GRIEVANCE PROCEDURE—The sole and exclusive procedure available to all employees in a particular bargaining unit and the employer for processing grievances and disputes.

NET ASSETS—Total assets minus total liabilities.

NET INCOME—The excess of all revenues and gains for a period over all expenses and losses of the same period.

NET LOSS—The excess of all expenses and losses for a period over all revenues and gains of the same period.

NET WORTH—Property owned, i.e.—assets—minus debts and obligations owed—i.e., liabilities—is the owner's net worth—i.e., equity.

NOTES AND ACCOUNTS RECEIVABLE—A secured or unsecured receivable evidenced by a note or open account arising from activities involving liquidation and disposal of loan collateral.

ORDINARY INTEREST—Simple interest based on a year of 360 days, contrasting with exact interest having a base year of 365 days.

ORGANIZATIONAL CHART—A linear direction of responsibility and authority within a company or institution.

OUTLAYS—Net disbursements for administrative expenses and for loans and related costs and expenses.

PARTNERSHIP—A legal relationship existing between two or more persons contractually associated as joint principals in a business.

PATENT—A patent secures the exclusive right to make, use and sell an invention for 17 years.

PIERCING THE CORPORATE VEIL—The process of holding another liable, such as an individual, for the acts of a corporation.

PRIME RATE—Interest rate which is charged business borrowers having the highest credit ratings, for short term borrowing.

PRODUCT LIABILITY—Type of tort or civil liability that applies to product manufacturers and sellers.

PROFESSIONAL ASSOCIATIONS—Non-profit, cooperative and voluntary organizations that are designed to help their members in dealing with problems of mutual interest.

PROFESSIONAL MALPRACTICE—The failure of one rendering professional services to exercise that degree of skill and learning commonly applied in the community by the average prudent reputable member of the profession, with the result of injury, loss or damage to the recipient of those services, or to those entitled to rely upon them.

PROFIT—Excess of revenues over expenses for a transaction.

PROFIT AND LOSS STATEMENT—Statement of income.

PROFIT MARGIN—Sales minus all expenses.

PROPRIETORSHIP—The most common legal form of business ownership comprising about 85 percent of all small businesses and whereby the liability of the owner is unlimited.

PRO-RATA BASIS—Proportionately.

PROSPECTUS—A document given by a company to prospective investors, which sets forth all the material information concerning the company and its financial stability, so the investor can make an informed decision on whether to invest in it.

PURCHASE ORDER—A document which authorizes a seller to deliver goods, and is considered an offer which is accepted upon delivery.

RATIO—Denotes relationships of items within and between financial statements, e.g., current ratio, quick ratio, inventory turnover ratio and debt/net worth ratios.

REFORMATION—An equitable remedy which calls for the rewriting of a contract involving a mutual mistake or fraud.

RESCISSION—The cancellation of a contract which returns the parties to the positions they were in before the contract was made.

RETURN ON INVESTMENT—The amount of profit—i.e., return—based on the amount of resources—i.e., funds—used to produce it.

SALE—An agreement to transfer property from the seller to the buyer for a stated sum of money.

SALE AND LEASEBACK—An agreement whereby the seller transfers property to the buyer who immediately leases the property back to the seller.

SCOPE OF EMPLOYMENT—Those activities performed while carrying out the business of one's employer.

SECONDARY MARKET—Those who purchase an interest in a loan from an original lender, such as banks, institutional investors, insurance companies, credit unions and pension funds.

SERVICE CORPS OF RETIRED EXECUTIVES (SCORE)—Retired, and working, successful business persons who volunteer to render assistance in counseling, training and guiding small business clients.

SHAREHOLDER—A person who owns shares of stock in a corporation or joint-stock company, also referred to as a stockholder.

SHERMAN ANTITRUST ACT—A federal statute passed in 1890 to prohibit monopolization and unreasonable restraint of trade in interstate and foreign commerce.

SILENT PARTNER—An investor in a business who is either unidentified to third parties, or who does not take an active role in day-to-day management of the business.

SMALL BUSINESS DEVELOPMENT CENTER (SBDC)—The SBDC is a university-based center for the delivery of joint government, academic, and private sector services for the benefit of small business and the national welfare which is committed to the development and productivity of business and the economy in specific geographical regions.

SMALL BUSINESS ADMINISTRATION (SBA)—Organization whose fundamental purpose is to aid, counsel, assists and protect the interest of small businesses.

SMALL BUSINESS CORPORATION—A corporation which satisfies the definition of I.R.C. §1371(a), §1244(c)(2) or both. Satisfaction of I.R.C. §1371(a) permits a Subchapter S election, while satisfaction of I.R.C. §1244 enables the shareholders of the corporation to claim an ordinary loss on the worthlessness of the stock.

SMALL BUSINESS INVESTMENT ACT—Federal legislation enacted in 1958 under which investment companies may be organized for supplying long term equity capital to small businesses.

SOLE PROPRIETORSHIP—A form of business in which one person owns all the assets of the business, and is solely liable for the debts of the business.

SPECIFIC PERFORMANCE—The equitable remedy requiring the party who breaches a contract to perform his or her obligations under the contract.

STOCK CERTIFICATE—A certificate issued to a shareholder which evidences partial ownership of the shareholder in a company.

STRICT LIABILITY—A concept applied by the courts in product liability cases, in which a seller is liable for any and all defective or hazardous products which unduly threaten a consumer's personal safety.

SUBLEASE—Transaction whereby tenant grants interests in leased premises less than his own, or reserves a reversionary interest in the term.

SUBSTANTIAL PERFORMANCE—The performance of nearly all of the essential terms of a contract so that the purpose of the contract has been accomplished giving rise to the right to compensation.

SUM CERTAIN—Liquidated damages pursuant to contract, promissory note, law, etc.

TAFT-HARTLEY ACT—Refers to the Labor-Management Relations Act of 1947, which was established to prescribe the legitimate rights of both employees and employers.

TARIFF—A form of tax assessed against imported and exported goods.

TIME IS OF THE ESSENCE—A clause in a contract which states that the specified time of performance is an essential term of the contract which, if breached, will serve to discharge the entire contract.

TRADE ASSOCIATION—An organization established to benefit members of the same trade by informing them of issues and developments within the organization and about how changes outside the organization will affect them.

TRADE CREDIT—Debt arising through credit sales and recorded as an account receivable by the seller and as an account payable by the buyer.

TRADEMARK—Refers to any mark, word, symbol or other device used by a manufacturer to identify its products.

TRUTH IN LENDING ACT—A federal law which requires commercial lenders to provide applicants with detailed, accurate and understandable information relating to the cost of credit, so as to permit the borrower to make an informed decision.

TURNOVER—As it pertains to a business, turnover is the number of times that an average inventory of goods is sold during a fiscal year or some designated period which measures the efficiency of a business.

UNCONSCIONABLE—Refers to a bargain so one-sided as to amount to an absence of meaningful choice on the part of one of the parties, together with terms which are unreasonably favorable to the other party.

UNDELIVERED ORDERS—The amount of orders for goods and services outstanding for which, the liability has not yet accrued.

UNFAIR LABOR PRACTICE—Any activities carried out by either a union or an employer which violate the National Labor Relations Act.

UNIFORM COMMERCIAL CODE (UCC)—The UCC is a code of laws governing commercial transactions which was designed to bring uniformity to the laws of the various states.

UNILATERAL CONTRACT—A contract whereby one party makes a promise to do or refrain from doing something in return for actual performance by the other party.

UNION SHOP—A workplace where all of the employees are members of a union.

USURIOUS CONTRACT—A contract that imposes interest at a rate which exceeds the legally permissible rate.

USURY—Interest which exceeds the legal rate charged to a borrower for the use of money.

VARIANCE—Permission to depart from the literal requirements of a zoning ordinance.

VENDOR—A seller.

VENTURE CAPITAL—Money used to support new or unusual commercial undertakings; equity, risk or speculative capital.

VOLUNTARY ARBITRATION—Arbitration which occurs by mutual and free consent of the parties.

WARRANTY—An assurance by one party to a contract that a certain fact exists and may be relied upon by the other party to the contract.

WARRANTY OF FITNESS FOR A PARTICULAR PURPOSE—A warranty that goods purchased are suitable for the specific purpose of the buyer.

WARRANTY OF MERCHANTABILITY—A warranty that goods purchased are fit for the general purpose for which they are being purchased.

WORKERS' COMPENSATION—A state-mandated form of insurance covering workers injured in job-related accidents.

WORKING CAPITAL—Current assets minus current liabilities.

ZONE OF EMPLOYMENT—The physical area within which injuries to an employee are covered by worker compensation laws.

ZONING—The government regulation of land use.

BIBLIOGRAPHY AND ADDITIONAL READING

Applegate, Jane Succeeding in Small Business. New York, NY: The Penguin Group, 1992.

Black's Law Dictionary, Fifth Edition. St. Paul, MN: West Publishing Company, 1979.

Clark, Scott A. Beating the Odds, 10 Smart Steps to Small Business Success. New York, NY: American Management Association, 1991.

Davidson, Jeffrey P. Avoiding the Pitfalls of Starting Your Own Business. New York, NY: Walker Publishing Company, Inc., 1988.

DuBoff, Leonard D. The Law For Small Businesses. New York, NY: John Wiley & Sons, Inc., 1991.

Employer's Alert, Federal Immigration Reform and Control Act of 1990, How to Comply Without Discriminating. New York State Department of Economic Development.

Equal Employment Opportunity Commission (Date Visited: April 2001) <http://www.eeoc.gov/>.

Hancock, William A. The Small Business Legal Advisor. New York, NY: McGraw-Hill, Inc., 1992.

Lasser, J.K. How To Run A Small Business. New York, NY: Simon & Schuster, Inc., 1989.

Parson, Mary Jean Financially Managing the One-Person Business. New York, NY: The Putnam Publishing Group, 1991.

Rubin, Richard L., and Goldberg, Philip The Small Business Guide to Borrowing Money. New York, NY: McGraw-Hill, Inc., 1980.

Small Business Administration (Date Visited: April 2001) <http://www.sba.gov/>.

Social Security Administration (Date Visited: April 2001) <http://www.ssa.gov/>.

United States Government Electronic Commerce Policy (Date Visited: April 2001) <http://www.ecommerce.gov/>